NATIONAL LIBRARY OF U.S.A.

MASTERPIECES OF SCULPTURE FROM THE NATIONAL GALLERY OF ART

ASPECTS OF THE WESTERN TRADITION

1200 · 1900

MASTERPIECES OF SCULPTURE

FROM THE

NATIONAL GALLERY OF ART

BY

CHARLES SEYMOUR, JR.

NATIONAL GALLERY OF ART
SMITHSONIAN INSTITUTION, WASHINGTON, D. C.

COWARD-McCANN, INC. · NEW YORK

N
856
A663

10/5/53 Gift

Copyright 1949

PUBLICATIONS FUND

NATIONAL GALLERY OF ART

WASHINGTON, D. C.

MANUFACTURED IN THE UNITED STATES OF AMERICA • PRODUCED BY THE BECK ENGRAVING COMPANY

34016

FOREWORD

By David E. Finley
Director, National Gallery of Art

One of the aims of the National Gallery of Art is to illustrate, in its collections, the development of the Western tradition in the fields of painting, sculpture and the graphic arts. Another aim, no less important, is to make the works of art in its collections known and enjoyed by as many people as possible. In order to further these aims, the National Gallery is publishing this book, which is intended to provide a representative view of the Gallery's present resources in the field of sculpture and to serve as a companion volume to the "Masterpieces of Painting from the National Gallery of Art," published in 1944.

By a fortunate combination of circumstances, the Mellon, Kress, and Widener Collections came to the National Gallery at the time it was founded or shortly afterwards. All contain outstanding works by many of the world's greatest sculptors. As a result the National Gallery, although it has been open to the public less than nine years, is now in the front rank of museums showing sculpture, especially of the Renaissance period. The Gallery also contains fine examples illustrating the major trends in sculpture immediately preceding and following the Renaissance. In this respect the Gallery's collection of sculpture parallels its collection of paintings, which covers the period from the thirteenth to the twentieth century.

With the growth of public collections in this country and Europe during the last hundred years, there has come inevitably a new appraisal of the quality and significance of sculpture shown in our museums. Twentieth-century concern for the primitive, the archaic, expressionism and abstraction, has tremendously enhanced the appeal of medieval art. And in these days when an alien, retrogressive and materialist philosophy seeks to dominate our world, the art of the Renaissance seems to us infinitely desirable with its emphasis on spiritual values and the importance of man as an individual. We turn with relief and with nostalgic longing to the Renaissance for the supreme expression of humanism in Western sculpture and for contact with the great creative minds of that turbulent and self-confident era in human history. Such contact can help us to understand and solve the artistic and moral problems of our own day and thus to benefit by the great legacy which has come to us from the past.

This book is designed to bring closer to us the vital aspects of that legacy and to make us familiar with some of the treasures now assembled in Washington.

ACKNOWLEDGMENTS

The photographs on pages 62, 63, 72, 73, 77-79, 99-101, 109-116 and 120 are by Professor Clarence Kennedy of Smith College, reproduced here by his permission and by that of Duveen Brothers, Inc., who also made available the photographs on pages 57, 80, 81 and 119. The remainder of the photographs are by Henry B. Beville, Chief Photographer at the National Gallery of Art.

Many conclusions concerning individual pieces stem from research done by Hanns Swarzenski, now of the Boston Museum of Fine Arts, while he was Acting Curator of Sculpture at the Gallery during the last war and while we worked together after the war; I would like to express appreciation of his contribution and also to take responsibility for any errors or misjudgments which may appear in the text, which was not actually written until after his departure. I want to thank for patient reading and suggested revisions of the text Huntington Cairns, Secretary; John Walker, Chief Curator; and J. B. Eggen, former Editorial Consultant and Adviser—all of the National Gallery of Art. The late Stephen S. Pichetto, Consultant Restorer of the National Gallery of Art, and Wilhelm Suida, Consultant to the Kress Foundation, have made suggestions which have been incorporated. I wish particularly to acknowledge the judgment, enthusiasm and encouragement of David E. Finley, Director of the National Gallery of Art and of Harry A. McBride, Administrator and Chairman of the Publications Committee of the Gallery.

C. S., Jr.

LIST OF PLATES

Descriptive notes on the pieces illustrated: pages 171-184

INTRODUCTION

Masterpieces are created by tradition as well as by individuals. The original meaning of *masterpiece* was specialized. It designated an object which qualified a young worker in the arts for the title of master in a medieval guild. The guild itself, like its successor and rival the humanistic art academy, was a powerful instrument of tradition. As a continuing institution, it "handed on" from one generation to the next a body of principles and attitudes toward the making of art. It could provide a foundation, a basis of information and training—a platform—from which a man of genius might rise to create the consummate examples of craft and imagination which later periods came to call masterpieces in a rather looser interpretation of the original meaning of the word.

That interpretation is even looser today. A masterpiece may mean simply an unusually fine example of a style or period, rather than an absolute summit of achievement. Even so, the older relationship with tradition persists. For a masterpiece is not recognized until it is seen against a large background. It arises through comparison with other related work; it also seems to require an origin in a movement in art so well established that its principles have ceased to be considered experimental and have become instead a recognized system of acquired values.

In baldest terms, a tradition in art is an enduring system of values. Thus a tradition, for example the familiar "Greek Tradition" in art, may appear to have form; it suggests structure. It is more than the sum of works of art created in a certain locality over a certain period of time. It implies a spirit, or point of view, or a method of approach. It has continuity, and within certain limits, unity. It grows, wanes, apparently disappears, revives. A tradition maintains procedures of technique. It also maintains standards of workmanship and artistic objectives. Even when tradition is sharply broken, it is still a point of departure and may remain to color and modify the boldest experiments.

We are concerned here with aspects of the tradition of Western sculpture from the twelfth century to approximately the year 1900. It is a European tradition which grows out of the art of the classical Mediterranean; but it would be wrong to think of it as merely a continuation of classical Antiquity. Between Antiquity and the developed phases of medieval European art stand nearly five centuries, called in many ways erroneously the "Dark Ages," yet nevertheless a time when the art of large-scale monumental sculpture in bronze and stone all but completely disappeared in Western Europe.

What I am calling the Western tradition is based on a period of experiment, of what amounts to a re-invention of sculpture, in medieval times, growing and expanding during the Renaissance and productive of a vast quantity of admirable and lovely art

Pages 27, 30, 42 in the seventeenth, eighteenth and nineteenth centuries. Survivals of the older Barbarian and late Antique traditions put forward precious metals and precious stones as desirable media; and some of the finest things in Western sculpture are sometimes classed as Pages 33, 55, 58, 73, 82 jewelry or goldsmith work. Stone however, especially white marble, and bronze provided the chief materials, but there was room too for limestone, terra cotta and wood, very frequently painted. Even after sculpture ceased to be painted in the principal European centers, a predominately optical or visual approach continued. Here is one of Pages 105, 155 the sources of unity in the Western tradition to 1900, apparently lying behind the illusionistic relief styles of the Renaissance and the coloristic effects even in the whitest of marbles by later European sculptors. It is thus a tradition which conceives of sculpture less often in terms of touch than of sight and vision. Beginning with visions of religion Pages 27, 67, 161, 168 it has tended to reinforce mankind's most optimistic visions of himself, of his importance, of his dignity and essential beauty, without forgetting his humanity. This has led to original and extremely varied interpretations of man's image in combination with underlying abstract elements of form, all in function of light, space, weight and density.

Seen in this way, the traditional sculpture of the Western world is more than patterned relationships of solids and voids. It is not only a perpetual challenge to thought and sensitivity; it may also be symbolic of man's effort to control his environment and himself. Toward the year 1500 it was possible for one theorist, Pomponio Gaurico, to say of statuary: ". . . it is to this one art that all the others tend, and are related, even as other arts and sciences are related to Philosophy herself."

The commentary which follows is in no sense a history. It suggests through a selected number of works of art changes in Western European sculpture which eventually resulted in the definition of sculpture chiefly as statuary in Pomponio Gaurico's period. And from that extreme definition of the aims of sculpture, in which the idealized free-standing image of man was considered the measure of all art, it is possible to sense later elaborations and variations leading through the Baroque, the eighteenth century and the nineteenth century to a point where continuity begins to falter and Western sculpture will seek differing paths.

Medieval Sculpture

The earliest piece of medieval sculpture in the National Gallery of Art might escape the casual eye—it is not on a pedestal, but in its original position, as it should be, as an integral part of a monument. That "monument" is the *Chalice of Suger,* once in the Page 27 treasury of St. Denis and made toward the middle of the twelfth century on the order of Abbot Suger, who might be called the founder of both the French national monarchy and Gothic architecture.

As seen here, considerably enlarged, the central medallion on the foot of Suger's chalice might decorate a portal of a great church. If one is doubtful as to what "monumentality" in sculpture means, this enlargement should help to give an answer. With feeling for a grand scale, the conventional treatment of the face and hands increases an expression of majesty, of wonder and the mystery of unearthly things. It shows a tremendously complex synthesis of older classical, Eastern and Barbarian styles. Historically, it is a point of departure for more naturalistic phases of artistic expression over the succeeding centuries. But whatever the value of those later phases may be, one has the feeling that it can be achieved only at the expense of losing a kind of plastic authority and a certain artistic wisdom present here.

Something of the same impressiveness is to be seen in the secular water vessel in *Page 28* the shape of a lion, probably from Northeast France toward the year 1200. Some of the stylizations, especially of the mane, have much earlier origins—the comparison with a finely cast bronze Sienese version of the well-known Etruscan *Wolf of the Capitoline* shows certain correspondences in this aspect which suggest the strength of formal tradition *Pages 29, 31* and provide a meeting place for the Middle Ages, Antiquity and the Renaissance. The lion, however, is built up on far more imaginative theory; its body is patterned after a bull and its general effect is of a hybrid monster. It contains a residue of the Barbarian ornamental animal style. With the *Wolf* we are closer to observed reality; its stylization is less ornamental and remote. It emphasizes the nature of the subject as a wild beast, associated nevertheless with human civilization, and so successfully that it has become through repetition one of the classic images of the West.

Development along stylized lines in medieval sculpture appears in another slightly later North European aquamanile. Here the limits between abstract and representational forms are nearly reached, but the style is effective since its abstract forms correspond *Pages 32, 33* to its function as a water vessel. The figure is in the form of a favorite medieval motive—the rider. The almost limitless possibilities of variation on the theme can be sensed in the succeeding plates. One in particular, an English alabaster of Saint George, shows a related emphasis on smooth rounded volumes and broad curves; but there is a *Page 36* note of pageantry, here echoed by the gay polychromy of the original painted accents still largely intact. On the reverse of a medal by Pisanello, done perhaps a generation *Page 37* later than the Saint George, there is a like feeling for pageantry mingled with the humane and religious values of chivalry. The proportions of both horse and knight in Pisanello's design are closer to nature than in the English alabaster, and the artist shows more interest in the casual appearances of nature in his foreshortening of the horse and suggestion of a rocky landscape. These characteristics point toward the Renaissance, but the underlying spirit of the two pieces is still essentially medieval.

A more remote spirit is felt in the unusual medals of Heraclius and Constantine, for which a Burgundian origin has been suggested. These are more tenuous in the proportions *Pages 38, 39* of the figures and nervous in drapery style, as befits a late refined phase of Northern medieval art; but the medals contain, nevertheless, premonitions of the Early Renaissance in several details—the horse of the equestrian Emperor, the cart suggesting a "Trionfo," the profile portrait, and Neoplatonic analogies connected with light and love.

Pages 40, 42 A further group of plates centered around the solemn theme of the Trinity makes possible more comparisons. Enlargement in the camera has again revealed the quality of the first of these: the central portion of an ecclesiastical brooch, or morse, removed in this instance from its frame. The technique is gold enamel, extremely delicate in its modeling, in high favor about the year 1400 in the royal and ducal courts of France. The *Pages 43-45* grandeur of the theme is realized in the figure of the Father, which has all the impressive scale of a prophet by Claus Sluter. The contrast with the alabaster *Trinity*, for which an English origin has been proposed, begins with technique: in mass and in the modeling of the head, this is mason's sculpture hewn from a block, which is still suggested in the pose and volumes, preserving the bigness and strength of the architecture to which it is related in style. The emotion is almost entirely concentrated on the Christ; the Father remains impassive, the features reminiscent of High Gothic cathedral sculpture.

Pages 46-48 In the *Trinity with Christ Supported by an Angel*, by an Upper-Rhenish master of the first quarter of the fifteenth century, the tragic figure of Our Lord assumes the dominant position: the Angel is present only to support the pathetically drooping figure of the dead Christ, the Father is symbolized only by the hand emerging from clouds. It is but a step to the representation of Christ alone supported by angels or alone with the symbols of the Passion—the process is a personalizing and humanizing of a doctrine, with emphasis growing on the suffering, in human terms, of the God of the Incarnation. The sculpture trembles here between vision and reality—between convention and naturalism as seen in the contrasting treatment of the stylized ribs and realistic belly of the principal figure. It has the preciousness of ivory, yet some of the large-scale form of architectural carving.

Because of the very nature of her humanity and her role of intercessor between man and Divinity, there are probably more representations of the Virgin in Gothic sculpture than of any other theme. Two Italian medieval carvings reveal an interesting *Pages 49-52* contrast of presentation and throw light on one of the most critical moments in all the development of Western sculpture. The first is by the fourteenth-century Sienese, Tino di Camaino. The graceful, swinging rhythms are not unlike the contemporary fourteenth-century style in Sienese painting. The composition of the relief must be seen frontally and repeats the design of many a devotional panel. There is a loss of power, in sculptural terms, in comparison with earlier work. But the change corresponds to new needs of expression. One senses a certain polish and impersonality, a certain courtliness. The relief was ordered by a Queen, and the Madonna is shown as a Queen in her court.

Pages 53-56 In Jacopo della Quercia's *Madonna of Humility*, the sculptural image is again parallel to Sienese painting; the idea of the Madonna seated on the ground in token of her humility was popularized in Italy and enters Western art, as far as can be judged, in Sienese painting of the fourteenth century. How Quercia's early style could have grown out of the earlier Sienese tradition of sculpture is also evident. But here, on the threshold of the Quattrocento, there is a new search for plastic power. There is also a suggestion of a proud classical Vesta as well as of a Duccio Madonna in the features of the Virgin. The interior rhythms are built on a twisting curve. The group composes from several angles—it is hard to find a view which can be called "front" or "principal" view. Such anticipations of developed Renaissance style are expressed in a language which is still clearly medieval. Here is an object lesson in the dangers of setting up overrigorous divisions between "periods" in the history of art. Where can a precise line be drawn between "Middle Ages" and "Renaissance"?

Pages 53, 54
Page 56

Early Tuscan Renaissance

The influence of Quercia's later style can be felt in two Florentine Madonnas with the Child which have been attributed to Ghiberti and Donatello. Both of terra cotta and both painted, they represent a type of imagery and style which grew up alongside stone and metalwork in the early decades of the Quattrocento. These Madonnas answer to the same taste and have much in common. There is a relation of more than cousinship in the two boys. And in the Madonnas there is a kindred expression of naturalism, mingled with an appealing winsomeness and a certain grandeur—perhaps a reinterpretation of the more formalized elegance in medieval Madonna types. Of the two, the standing Madonna is more advanced in style and more cohesive in design. The composition handles successfully a series of related curves which move in all three dimensions.

Pages 58, 59
Pages 60, 61

The contrast with the glazed terra-cotta Madonna, ascribed to another and somewhat misunderstood Florentine sculptor, Michelozzo, is in more than technique. The white glaze, familiar in the work of the Robbia family, is both protection for the terra-cotta surface and imitation of polished marble. One can debate the taste which gave this glazing technique its popularity. But here, while the glaze may clog many delicate passages, it has none of the cold, mechanical quality of the usual Robbia shopwork. The glazing here appears to be experimental, and its very faults of unevenness provide for modern eyes an added element of quality. The deep tenderness in the relationship between the Mother and Child is expressed in an unusually direct way. The style is clearly beyond the mannerism of late Gothic art, and in its mingling of realism and classical idealism anticipates to some extent the nineteenth century. Its spirit, however, is considerably more than modern sentiment. Notice how the motive of the limply hanging arm of the Child, which occurs only as a secondary descriptive detail in the standing Madonna, is brought directly into the foreground of the design. It is used not as genre-motif, but as a sculptural expression of density and weight; it functions not only as a memory of visually perceived reality, but as an element of drama, and reinforces the idea, characteristic of medieval and Early Renaissance religious thought, that the Infant's sleep prefigures the death of the Saviour.

Pages 64, 65
Pages 59, 63, 64

It may appear surprising to see in these Madonnas in terra cotta how close Donatello is to Ghiberti and how far, essentially, he is from his partner, Michelozzo. One might expect the opposite. There is always the difficulty of pinning down what is meant by "Donatello's style." It is not enough to say that it is a combination of realism and classicism, or that it is a reflection of the conflict of medieval spirit with the new materialism of the Early Renaissance. The artist in Donatello must have been very complex. He seems to have felt form in its largest unities, and yet he was unable to express himself with a corresponding directness. There is in his work a kind of mannerism, a conscious effort toward style, which may vary in intensity but never yields a really lucid statement. One can never tire of the experience of trying to find the secret of his sculpture.

There is given here a partial photographic survey of one of Donatello's most enigmatic and yet truly grandiose marbles—the *David of the Casa Martelli.* Conjectures as to its date and the meaning of the chisel marks on its surface have been numerous and contradictory. *Pages 66, 67* But it should be obvious that we have here something which is neither immature nor unsuccessful. It is experimental, certainly, and in strange ways. The pose is original, but appears to be a deliberate distortion of the classical Antique formula of balance. *Page 66* The head is inspired from the Antique, but has a new and very haunting intensity which does not result from naturalism or portraiture alone. *Page 70* The proportions must originally have been conceived as heavier — the figure must have been fuller and stockier. One can trace revisions in the arms, on the right leg and around the waist; they were never carried to a new completion. But on the head of Goliath, so like that of a *Page 71* Dying Gaul, the similar broad chisel-strokes could hardly be refined without loss of *Page 69* vitality. Close by are the delicate leaves of plants outlined in low relief against the supporting tree trunk. The statue is alive with contrasts. It is a figure balanced between awkwardness and grace, between childhood and maturity, between the heroic and the intimate, alert yet in repose. It hovers between realism, classicism and the invention of a poet.

Pages 72, 73 Donatello's strange emotional genius is reflected in a polychrome bust representing Saint John the Baptist, where the subtle void of the open mouth is contrasted with the half-closed introspective eyes, and the tumbled hair with the enamel-like finish of the flesh. This is an example of psychological study; it is an historically significant attempt to portray the inner life of an ascetic and mystic—the "eater of locusts" of the Biblical text, the "voice of one crying in the wilderness." The subject is really that "voice."

The bust-form is characteristic of Renaissance sculpture. It is all too easy to see in it a connection with the general revival of the Antique, where the bust is a basic element of sculpture. But it is difficult to discover why so many of the busts of the Early Renaissance differ so from the usual Antique formula, or indeed, how and where the Quattrocento first made use of the form. It is certainly true that the Middle Ages used the bust, in isolated cases inspired from classical models, and frequently enough in reliquaries. These Western medieval forms may well have colored the Quattrocento development.

But for the Early Renaissance sculptors, the interest in the bust-form must have been encouraged by constant rediscovery and revaluation of Antique remains. In their hands it becomes a very useful means of studying humanity within the expressive focus of the head; the shoulders then provide a plinth and an opportunity in costume or ornament to suggest additional characterization or symbolism.

A group of plates illustrating three busts of boys will make evident the originality and freshness of Quattrocento sculpture. *Pages 75, 77, 78* Few subjects are more difficult to portray than childhood, especially for the sculptor. Yet in the two busts of boys, the delicacy of the contours, the tenderness of modeling, the transitions between the planes and volumes appear effortless. One must be attentive to realize that there are qualities of structure behind the charm of manner and anecdotal reporting of appearances. As Vasari wrote in the sixteenth century of Desiderio's extraordinary facility . . . . "This is a truly heavenly gift which bestows upon [his] works such a light and graceful appearance that they attract not only those who understand the profession, but also many others . . . ." It is interesting to note that Desiderio did not succumb to a formula. Both children represent the Christ Child, but there are subtle but very real differences of style in the two *Pages 74, 79* heads, which on first glance appear almost identical: the one solemn, quiet, with a suggestion of pathetic fragility, the other creating a mood of gaiety caught with lighter touches of the chisel.

Scholars are still engaged in separating the artistic personality of Desiderio da Settignano from that of his master, Donatello. For a long time, the two busts of boys discussed above were considered as by Donatello, and the traditional attribution of the *Pages 80, 81* third bust, *The Young Saint John the Baptist,* in our group of three boys, was to Donatello also. The presence of a hand which is neither that of Donatello nor Desiderio is at once apparent in the different conception of childhood and in construction of form. The current attribution is to Antonio Rossellino. But if the bust is by him, it shows an unusual feeling for serenity. The quality of the modeling of the surfaces, creating what appears to be an atmospheric veil around the features, seems to remove the work from the world of normal activity, reinforces the attitude of contemplation and withdrawal. This quality, together with the generalized and idealized features, suggests the sculpture of fourth-century Greece. It is not, however, an archeological classicism, nor is it academic; but it is moving toward the relative generalization and simplification which are among the characteristics of early Cinquecento classic style.

Pages 82-90 present three Quattrocento ladies. We do not know, with certainty, who they were in life. That these are portraits seems unquestioned. A generation or so ago, it seemed to scholars very important to identify the sitters. But today, they all appear, in different ways, to express a type—a kind of style of elegance and beauty. This creates a gulf between us and their personalities more difficult to cross than that caused by the loss of documents needed to establish, with absolute certainty, their identities. *Pages 82, 86* There can be sensed, even so, in these Renaissance ladies, a considerable variety within the mold of fashion. Compare the alertness and youth in the first with the dignity of the second. The latter, incidentally, comes more alive in profile or three-quarters rear view, and *Pages 84, 85* in both the exquisite carving of the backs reveals that they were thought of as completely in the round.

The third lady in the group differs in style. It is not by a Florentine, but by a very interesting itinerant artist, Francesco da Laurana, who came somewhat under Florentine influence in his travels from Dalmatia to the courts of Naples and Provence. He is *Pages 87, 89, 90* revealed here in his most Florentine phase. But his feeling for relatively simple, geometric volumes, combined in pervasive repetitions, is far more abstract than Desiderio's. The artistic climate of Naples in 1475, where this portrait of a Princess was carved, was far more medieval than in Florence, and the stylized forms used by Laurana would probably have seemed flaccid to Florentine taste. Laurana's portrait rather begs the question so urgently posed by Donatello, which is essentially the problem of retaining the vitality of nature when natural forms are submitted to dramatic devices or stylizing *Page 87* disciplines. The delightful little reliefs of centaurs and *putti* on the base seem to reflect still another approach to form; they must have been taken directly from the Antique.

This leads us to another category of sculptural presentation, namely, relief. The Renaissance was fascinated by its problems, and in relief sculpture it is possible to find a meeting place for Renaissance theory in painting, sculpture, and architecture. The Quattrocento opens with the famous competition for the reliefs on the Florentine Baptistry doors, and it ends with Michelangelo's *juvenilia* in relief carving. Early Renaissance relief sculpture shows a great range and plays imaginatively between the limits of high relief verging on the full round and the most delicate suggestions of form that seem, at first glance, hardly more than a breath on the background plane. There is an elusive element of sophistication in Early Renaissance relief styles. The sculptor suggests depth or volume which does not actually exist. But it is not the illusion in itself which is sophisticated so much as the sureness and variety of method in producing effects. Three examples illustrate this observation.

Page 92 The first, a *Madonna and Child* by Agostino di Duccio, suggests volumes which seem to be sinking back into the stone from which they are carved, to find the uniform *Page 91* surface of a painting. When looked at from the side, the relief reveals a curious set of distortions; they are rather like devices of foreshortening in drawing, producing, when seen from the front, the illusion of volume which they do not in themselves possess. Carried to these lengths, this type of carving does not appear to be dependent on models of *Page 94* classical Antique relief style; it seems to owe far more to the influence of contemporaneous painting. In the composition and human types, it suggests a connection with such a painter as Fra Filippo Lippi, or the early phase of Botticelli.

A similar connection with painting is revealed in the extraordinary and very sensi- *Pages 95-97* tive *Virgin Annunciate*, attributed to Mino da Fiesole. In this case, the analogy is with Sienese, rather than Florentine painting. The relief is on the verge of sculpture in the full-round, and yet it remains a relief; it assumes the form of a bust and yet shrinks from the possession of space, which the prouder ladies by Desiderio assume, as if by right. More characteristic of Mino are the full-length figures of *Faith* and *Charity,* where feeling, material, and style of execution unite in subtle yet convincing elegance. Pages 98-101

Developed Florentine pictorial relief is well illustrated in the composition presenting Saint Jerome in the Desert by Desiderio. Pages 102-105 The general style harks back to Ghiberti and to some aspects of Donatello, but the delicate handling of the transitions of plane and volume are characteristic of a later hand. Sculpture here obviously approaches painting very closely. This is a "scene"; it takes place within a rectangular frame which can be hung on a wall. Page 102 We find in Renaissance inventories, like those of the Medici Palace, the word *quadro,* which can refer indiscriminately to a painting or to a relief of this kind. In this particular relief, the illusion of space is subtly modulated. Ghiberti's early systematic clarity, depending upon the definition of three zones (foreground, middle ground, and background) with corresponding heights or levels of relief, is dissolved into a much vaguer unity with transitions that escape close analysis. The sensitivity of technique would appear to deny the hardness of the material, and yet one feels the marble everywhere.

This quality is nowhere more evident than in the running figure to the right in *stiacciato,* or extremely low relief, for which the Florentines were famous. Page 103 Such carving is an index of the highest manual dexterity, but its real artistic significance is elsewhere. It consists primarily, in sculptor's terms, in the combination of opposites: the freedom of suggested volumes with the surface-tension of the flat background plane. It is a kind of sculptural paradox. Similar effects can be found in the carved decoration of glass or crystal. Carved crystals, as well as transparent gems were available to the Florentine sculptors, and the glyptic effects in much of *stiacciato* relief may have resulted from their study and adaptation to non-transparent materials, as in this marble.

I can think of no better way to suggest the sculptural quality of this aspect of pictorial relief: its precision, its formal subtlety and its ultimate independence from the illusionism of atmospheric distance in painting. *Stiacciato* in this sense is, I believe, a peculiarly Florentine manifestation. Pages 106, 107 Low relief in Sienese sculpture of the same period is far less precise. There the effects are much richer in substance and surfaces; the design is less clear in outline and in the definition of interior volumes within the outline, more lyrical and less exact. It is somewhat the same difference, but with other points of emphasis, which has been noted for some time in comparative study of Florentine and Sienese painting.

Sienese relief, particularly in the work of Francesco di Giorgio, its finest exponent, differs considerably from Florentine relief-style in its handling of space. In Siena an architectural background is treated more as a fantasy than as part of a rationalized environment for human action. Page 106 At times a landscape, delicate and unreal, with no recognizable aim in defining space as a platform or as volume of atmosphere, provides a

Page 107 backdrop to the figure. At other times figures are set against a neutral plane which suggests space only in the unevennesses and half-accidental modeling of its surface. In examples like the last, a classical model can be supposed. But in the placement of the figures and above all in roughened, casual surfaces there is a feeling for form which opposes strongly the clarity, exactness and finish of high classical art.

One can debate the relative merits of classical prototype and Renaissance interpretation. But one eventually must concede that this Sienese style, in relation to the European art of its own time, is a very sophisticated kind of sculpture both in freedom of Page 108 modeling and choice of rich dark bronze for material. The relief of *Saint Sebastian* by Francesco di Giorgio contrasts in a striking way with the more provincial contemporary Pages 109, 110 style of Matteo Civitale, of Lucca. There the terra-cotta version of the same subject is smoothed into imitation of the actual appearance of the nude in nature. The application of naturalistic paint reinforces a lifelike quality in the body against which the artist appears to play a more poetic interpretation of saintly resignation and vision in the head.

By the last quarter of the fifteenth century, sculptural invention in Florence had turned from marble to bronze, terra cotta, and the search for plastic power in three full dimensions. It is, in many ways, a showier age than the previous generation, and one Pages 111, 112 feels in sculpture tendencies which parallel the energy, *Realpolitik,* and daring revealed by Lorenzo himself. In Verrocchio's charming terra-cotta *Putto Poised on a Globe,* there is a great deal more than its superficially frivolous subject matter would indicate. As a study of movement, the figure is particularly interesting. The various shifts of axes in the limbs and silhouette of the trunk are organized to make a balance—for example, there is a correspondence between the left arm and right leg, between the right arm and left leg. But this artificial balance is adapted not merely to naturalistic and picturesque forms of the fatty nude of infancy, but also to a dominant diagonal passing from the right hand to the left foot, which impels the figure forward and gives its movement character. This is a new conquest of space. The twisting curves of the design and the crisp contrasts of light and shade also suggest a significant shift of direction in sculptural style over the earlier formative period of Renaissance sculpture.

It would be difficult to find a more direct expression of this trend than in the portraits by Verrocchio of the Medici brothers, Giuliano and Lorenzo. Pages 114-116 The first is certainly the earlier, perhaps by almost a decade. It reveals the arrogance and brilliance of the younger Giuliano, and all the outward braggadocio of the Renaissance tyrant. The bust Pages 117-119 of Lorenzo, much heavier and on a larger scale, is far less picturesque in pose and in detail. The deep spatial shadows in the headdress are a kind of frame for the harsh mask, impressive not so much in its intrinsic ugliness of feature, as in its expression of implacable will power.

This Machiavellian aspect of the man is balanced by the profile view which reflects Page 119 instead, in a more fluent line and with less insistent masses, something of the poet and humanist in Lorenzo. It seems probable that Leonardo made a sketch of Verrocchio's bust of Lorenzo de' Medici, and it is interesting to note that it was the profile, not the full-face, which he recorded. Verrocchio represents the anti-classical wing of late Quattrocento sculpture; his vogue did not long survive Lorenzo, who died in 1492. His style represents a summing up of earlier trends; yet it is difficult to conceive of Michelangelo, and in some respects of seventeenth-century Baroque, without his experiments in energetic design, the drama of his handling of lights and darks, and his feeling for space as an environment for many-sided forms.

North-Italian and Later Renaissance Sculpture

Tuscany does not represent the entirety of the Early Renaissance, and the virtually exclusive stress which past criticism has laid upon Tuscan Quattrocento sculpture does not do justice to historical development in the Western tradition. During the fifteenth century, influence from Florence was largely limited to the Italian peninsula. The spread of the Renaissance style as a European phenomenon occurred later, after 1500, with its principal Italian sources in such centers as Rome, Milan or Venice rather than Florence or Siena. North-Italian sculpture is, consequently, more than a secondary school; it may be interpreted as a fertile meeting place for late medieval style and the humanist trends of Tuscan sculpture.

The mingling of Northern medieval and Tuscan humanist approaches is well illus- *Page 120*
trated in the medallion profile-portrait of Lodovico Sforza, ascribed to Amadeo. Amadeo himself is an interesting phenomenon; he is almost entirely lost today as an individual personality in a series of collaborative projects of architectural sculpture to which, like a Gothic master of the cathedral age, he gave his leadership. The Sforza portrait reflects the idealization of medieval art. It is a generalized expression of the calm power of a prince of Christendom, rather than an interpretation of the role of an ambitious tyrant to which Lodovico has been a little narrowly relegated by popularized history. The portrait was also intended to decorate a building. The cool simplicity of its design was to tell from an architectural setting, not too far from the eye of the observer and under not so glaring a light as to lose the delicate effects of modeling. Yet this portrait-form in stone derives directly from small-scale and more intimate medallic art.

The combination of public and private function in the Renaissance medal is perhaps its most interesting aspect from the point of view of its place in sculpture. The adaption of the form to monumental architectural design, as in the Amadeo Sforza portrait, is in reality only a development of an inherent capability. There is in early *Page 37*
North-Italian medallic art, evident particularly in Pisanello, a sense of structure and calm breadth of design which suggests a place on a monument of architecture. This char- *Page 121*
acteristic becomes the most evident in comparison with the intense and particularized portrait of Alberti, an extraordinary document from many points of view; this is probably not Pisanello's; recognition of its intellectual Florentine quality is reflected in the still tentative attribution to Alberti himself.

Pages 122, 123

As striking are the considerable differences between Tuscan and North-Italian marbles. The *Madonna* by Solari, which must be dated toward the end of the Quattrocento, may appear in comparison with the Madonnas of Agostino di Duccio or Desiderio to be a little clumsy and provincial. But there is a warmth and human quality which is lacking in comparable Florentine work, something of the quality to be found in the Madonnas of Giovanni Bellini's maturity. Similarly, there is a more human interpretation of classical forms in the *Singing Angel* by the Venetian, Pietro Lombardo. *Pages 124-126* Melancholy is balanced by a certain sprightliness; it is almost as if Mantegna, in an unusually lyric mood, had turned his hand to sculpture. It should be compared with the full-blown sixteenth-century classicism of the *Venus Anadyomene* by Jacopo Sansovino, *Pages 127-129* who, beginning in Florence and Rome, was to migrate after 1527 to Venice, where he was a dominant figure for most of the sixteenth century. Here it is Hellenistic Antiquity rather than Roman art dear to the severe genius of Mantegna that takes the upper hand. The heavy rounded forms of this *Venus* are already in harmony with the sensuous nudes of Titian.

The genius of North-Italian sculpture found its finest expression in bronze. Donatello's stay in Padua for ten years, between 1443 and 1453, was a starting point for a great school of Paduan bronze workers. It should be noted, however, that the development of the North-Italian school tended steadily away from the monumental aspects of Donatello's bronze style toward small-scale work with ever-increasing interest in Antique remains. The fusion of archaeological devotion to the Antique with intense emotion produced in Riccio, for one great example, a new and very powerful sculptural *Pages 130-132* expression in the West. His *Entombment*, shown here, is derived both from Roman sarcophagi in the composition of the figures, and from early Renaissance painting in the design of the landscape background. Riccio was the leader of his generation, but his influence was not so weighty as to preclude an enormous variety of personal styles both in Padua and in the related center of Venice.

Pages 133-135

One of these can be found in the group representing *Hercules and Antaeus*, ascribed to the Paduan, Francesco da Sant' Agata. While there are obvious connections with Riccio's style, the slender proportions of the figures and the bold extension of the pattern of flailing arms and legs show originality and, at the same time, a grasp of the possibilities of bronze in creating an open, space-devouring design. The opposition of the two figures is less a struggle than an episode in a dance. It is radically different from the close-bound muscular tension of Antonio Pollaiuolo's Florentine version of the same subject, done during the previous century; to compare the two is to realize, at least in part, the new elegance and, above all, feeling for space which comes in the sixteenth century under the heading of "Mannerism."

One of the little-stressed aspects of the sixteenth-century Mannerist movement is its romantic sensitivity, its lyric nostalgia for greater things; it seems to have suffered from a "mal du siècle," and its feeling for Antiquity is not unlike the Gothic Revival in nineteenth-century Romanticism. One has the impression that sixteenth-century sculpture, excluding possibly the maturity of Michelangelo, never quite lived up to the promise of its beginnings. Yet Mannerist sculpture poses in a vigorous way a great many of the formal problems which seem most interesting today. It is an art of expression and one also deeply attached to abstract form. A great deal of the sculptural tendencies of the sixteenth century was poured into painting. In looking at Florentine Mannerist portraits in painting, it is hard to say which is more sculptural: the sitter or the statuary frequently shown as an adjunct to the main figure. The shadow of Michelangelo, who was a sculptor even in his painting, fell heavily on his contemporaries and immediate successors.

Michelangelo's influence can be felt, as a reinterpretation but not an imitation, in a very distinguished Mannerist bronze—the *Descent from the Cross* by Vincenzo Danti. *Pages 136-138* The cast is unique and reproduces closely the fresh touches of the artist's hand. The relief plays freely from very high passages, some boldly emerging without transition from the middle planes, to suggestions of forms actually drawn on the background with a stylus. It offers many surprises to those who are accustomed to think of sixteenth-century sculpture in terms of "terribilità" or attempts at grandiosity. The detail of the fainting Virgin with the women about her reveals a sensitivity of feeling and rendering which *Page 137* is akin to the finest Romantic art. A more solid and more richly modeled style appears in Annibale Fontana's study for his marble *Adoration of the Shepherds*. *Pages 139-141* The freedom of the technique and the intimate scale of this terra cotta may appear to those who know the more academic marble in Milan to be far more appropriate to the artist's aims. The modeling of Giovanni da Bologna's *Mercury* is a product of the academic and perfectionist *Pages 142-145* phase of the sixteenth century. It has a little of the overemphasis on correctness, characteristic of the parvenu. Giovanni was a native of Flanders, but his style became so completely Italianized that one tends to forget the name Jehan de Boulogne, as he was originally called before he went to Italy. His career illustrates the "Europeanizing" of Renaissance art in the sixteenth century and the growth of a new international style. But over and above these historical considerations, the paradoxical buoyancy and precise rhythm of movement in the figure is a landmark in Western sculpture. Such qualities emphasize the very real contribution of Mannerist art.

Mannerist sculpture is not Baroque sculpture. But it prefigures in many ways the Baroque style. One can sense the Baroque as stirring into existence in the work of Adriaen de Vries, another Italianate Northerner who studied under Giovanni Bologna in *Pages 147, 149, 151* Italy and then returned to work primarily in Germanic territory. Proportions become heavier, the twist and contrapposto of sixteenth-century design turn into stronger and more pervasive reverse-curve rhythms. The fine-strung, nervous energy of the Mannerists develops into a broader and more confident power. The contrast of de Vries' *Virtue and Vice* of 1610 with a bronze of the same subject of approximately 1560-70 reflects the *Pages 146-149* difference not only between two personalities but between two phases of Western style.

After the Renaissance—Aspects of French Sculpture

Seventeenth-century Baroque sculpture is such an extreme interpretation of space and light, as well as of emotion, that the normal surroundings of nature and human environment do not easily stand its effects and in general do not show it off to true advantage. Baroque sculpture of this time grew up with artful constructions of nature in seventeenth-century gardens and fountains; it also grew up in the even more artful interpretation of light and space in seventeenth-century architecture. Partly because of this organic unity with man-made surroundings of its period, it is one of the styles in Western sculpture which most clearly approaches real invention. And this is the more remarkable because it was also a style which laid great stress on the mimicry of natural appearances.

Pages 152, 153

Page 153

A unique bronze version of Bernini's marble *Louis XIV* makes clear the development along picturesque and theatrical lines achieved by 1665 or shortly thereafter. The drapery is upheld and swirled by a fictitious breeze. The heavy curls of the full-bottom wig are treated very nearly as abstractions, as forms which exist only to suggest rich contrasts of light and shade or a harmony of linear curves with rounded volumes. The silhouette is broken into an extraordinary number of secondary patterns and lively rhythms. The arrogance of an individual is turned by some magic of this style into the very real grandeur of an absolute monarch.

Bernini was not the last Italian sculptor of value or interest, but his journey to France in 1665 was one of the last acts of Italian leadership in Western sculpture. Thereafter, in the eighteenth and nineteenth centuries, leadership fell to France. Most historians have stressed the differences between Bernini's outlook and the more academic classicism of his French contemporaries. Such differences undoubtedly existed, but they hardly serve to clarify the reason for a new charm and vitality which appears in French sculpture after Bernini's direct contact with French artists.

Page 154

Pages 156, 157

This novel trend in French sculpture was partially a result of the tastes of the Court, which determined the important commissions offered to sculptors. A large place, however, must be given to the very positive influence of Southern Baroque art. The effects of a mingling of Baroque elements with French classicism are to be seen in Jean Louis Lemoyne's *"Diana."* The design goes back to the decoration of the park at Marly in 1710 while Louis XIV was still alive; and there is in the figure a pastoral quality which was to color a great deal of French eighteenth-century art. The balance and calm of the composition with its clean-cut lines are characteristic of French classicism; but the picturesque pattern of the drapery and the suggestion of movement in the pose, and above all the pictorial effects of lights and darks in the head and face are reminiscent of Bernini's inventive style.

As the eighteenth century progressed, the Court style of Marly and Versailles altered, first toward increased elegance under the Regency and then under the late years of the reign of Louis XV and the early years of Louis XVI toward increasing realism mingled with a new classical revival. But the charm and freshness of the earlier Court style survived as a kind of miracle, just as something of the same quality lived on through French painting from Watteau through Fragonard. The apparent triviality of Clodion's subject matter should not conceal his very real talent for design and his capacity to create firmness in his volumes. One of a pair of ornamental urns, dated 1782, is classical in shape and contour but shows in an oval "cartouche" which decorates one side a great freedom in relief. This glimpse into the life of a family of satyrs is like the poetry of the humanistic Renaissance seen through the idealism of Rousseau or Bernardin de Saint-Pierre.

Pages 158, 159

Sculpture of this kind, which seems at first glance so simple and facile, is actually very complex. It is intimate in feeling and yet it admirably fulfills a monumental function; it combines romanticism with a certain realism; it is clearly classical in inspiration and yet introduces evident elements of contemporary delight in human experience; it is clever and intelligent without a trace of cynicism; it is agreeable without being superficial; it belongs very clearly to the eighteenth century, and yet it has a quality of universal meaning.

The greatest exponent of such a point of view is, of course, Houdon. His insistence was upon the dignity and intrinsic value of individual human beings. His sculpture seems to be the last superlative expression in the continuous tradition of European humanism. To compare Houdon's busts of the Brongniard children of approximately 1777 with Desiderio's boys is to find a certain companionship of spirit and in some respects of form. But one senses that for Houdon in 1777 (as for most of his contemporaries) childhood is important not so much for itself as for its relation to the adult human being who is to grow out of it. Desiderio seems to have been so enchanted with his discovery of the delicate forms of childhood that its deeper, eighteenth-century *philosophe* meaning at times seems to have escaped him. This immediate emphasis on observed nature speaks out in Desiderio, even though he was representing the Christ Child, a subject which one might think would place a tremendous premium on successful suggestion of the adult qualities of the Saviour. Houdon is less sentimental and cooler.

Pages 160-164

Page 74

Houdon lived on until 1828 and saw the triumph of Neoclassicism, familiar in the work of Canova. The so-called Romantic reaction against Neoclassicism which was well launched by 1850 seems far less extreme today than the Winckelmannesque spirit it fought. The Romantic movement in sculpture is a return to the principal stream of the Western tradition and also a return to earlier styles. Among them was the sculpture of the French eighteenth century. One aspect of Romantic sculpture is seen in the work of Carpeaux. The examples shown here, the *Neapolitan Fisherboy* and *Girl with a Shell*, reveal very plainly his debt to the spirit of eighteenth-century sculpture. But they also show a more exaggerated search for expression—an effort to bring warmth and suggested color into stone. In delicacy of play of light and shade and in subtlety of modeling Car-

Pages 166, 167

Page 165

peaux shows his interest in painting; he was an early exponent, although along parallel and somewhat independent lines, of French Impressionism. In the catching of a momentary glimpse of life about him and in the fixing of it in quick bold strokes of his brush or chisel his art is modern.

Carpeaux was one of Rodin's early teachers. Rodin thought in terms of more epic proportions than Carpeaux. In spite of his literary symbolism, which he overemphasized perhaps, there is a force and power, a surging vitality in his work which Western sculpture has rarely equaled. It is possible now to see those qualities more clearly and to revaluate his contribution. His effort to grasp form as unity rather than as a sum of a great many parts is one of his most modern characteristics. One feels it in his statue of Balzac, but even more clearly at times in his sketches in clay, which parallel his drawings. *Page 168* In a figure like the rather late reduced version of his *Age of Bronze*, the pose is clearly in the classical tradition, but romantic overtones of the subject (man awakening to a new age of civilization) bring in a strange and not easily forgotten dissonance with the classical elements in the design. In the treatment of the surfaces and such anatomical details as the muscles of the back or the eyes the sculptor simplifies, selects, rebuilds new forms; he consciously abstracts plastic meaning from those forms as found in nature and makes the observer conscious of the process. This is a prelude to another age of sculpture in the West, whose first avowed aim was to break with Rodin's romantic spirit and visual approach to sculptural form and to create an art on the basis of a new interpretation of the present and the past.

In leafing through the plates which follow the reader will, I believe, sense a unity as striking as the variety of styles. So vivid a union of stability and continuity with freedom of individual experiment is a rare phenomenon in the long history of art. The Western tradition of sculpture should for this reason alone always merit attention. Returning to the thought in the first paragraphs of this essay, I should like to emphasize its particular application to the sculpture of our Western past. A tradition in art is not a set of fixed conventions; nor is a tradition, or tradition in the generic sense, merely another synonym for group conservatism. Tradition is an element of order and continuity in life which may actually encourage as part of its structure and action an attitude of individual experiment. The Western tradition has placed an unusually high value on individual experiment in art. It has led us to treasure not "the artist" in general, but the personality and achievement of specific, individual human beings. And it has brought us to believe that each work of art is in itself a universe, unique and irreplaceable. Whatever may be the fate of the humanist values of the Western past, they will always be available in works of art such as those which are reproduced on the pages following. May the originals to which the photographs refer long be a source of wisdom and delight.

PLATES

Gold

Greatly Enlarged

FRENCH, c. 1140 · *Medallion of Christ Pantocrator on Suger's Chalice.* *Widener Collection.* See Note 1

Bronze, with traces of gilt

H. 5 7/16 in.

FRENCH, c. 1200 · *Lion, Aquamanile.* *Widener Collection.* See Note 2

Bronze

H. $14\frac{5}{16}$ in.

SIENESE, XV CENTURY · *The She-Wolf Nourishing Romulus and Remus.* *Kress Collection.* See Note 3

FRENCH, c. 1200 · *Lion, Aquamanile,* Detail. See Page 28

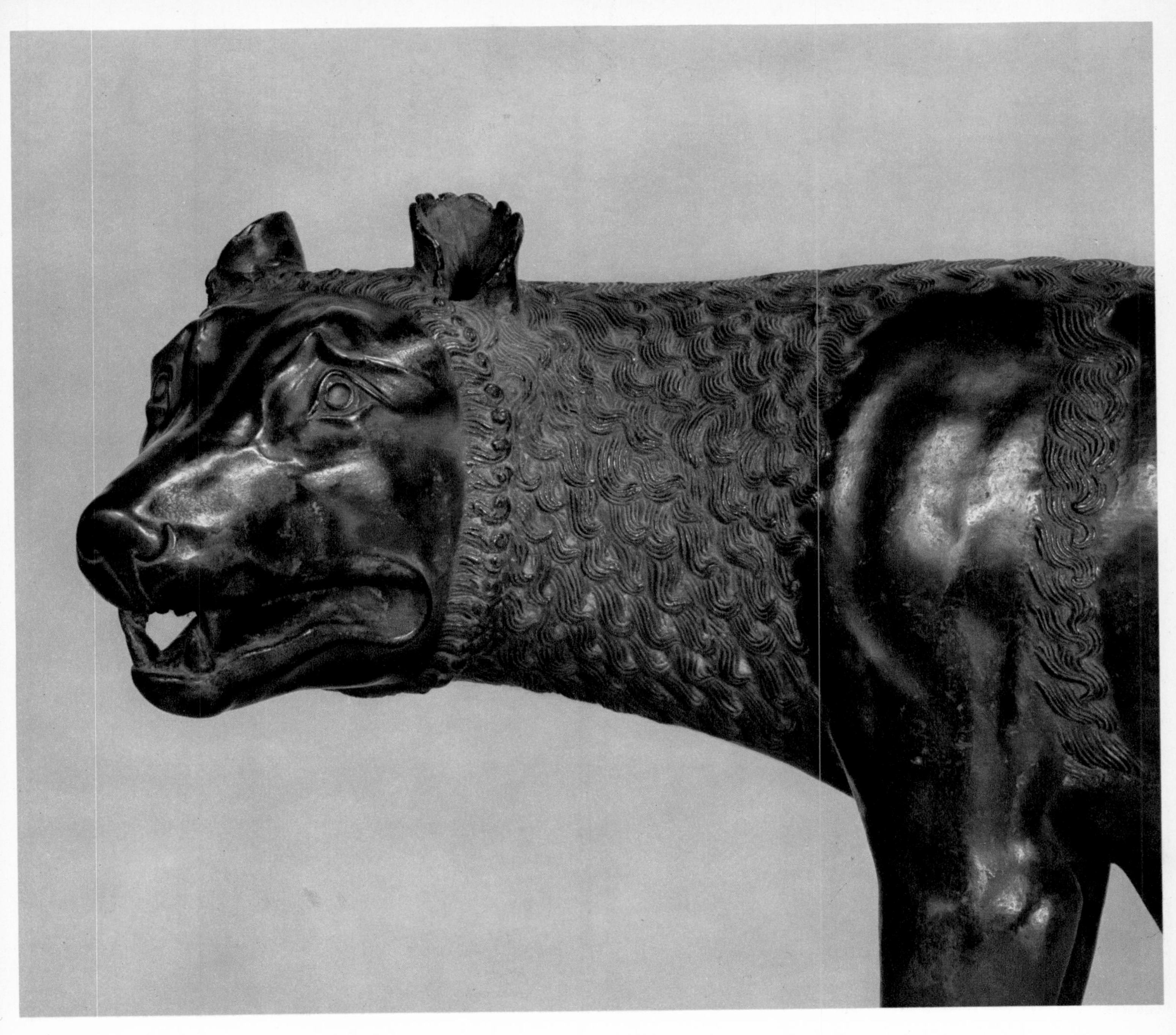

SIENESE, XV CENTURY · *The She-Wolf Nourishing Romulus and Remus,* Detail. See Page 29

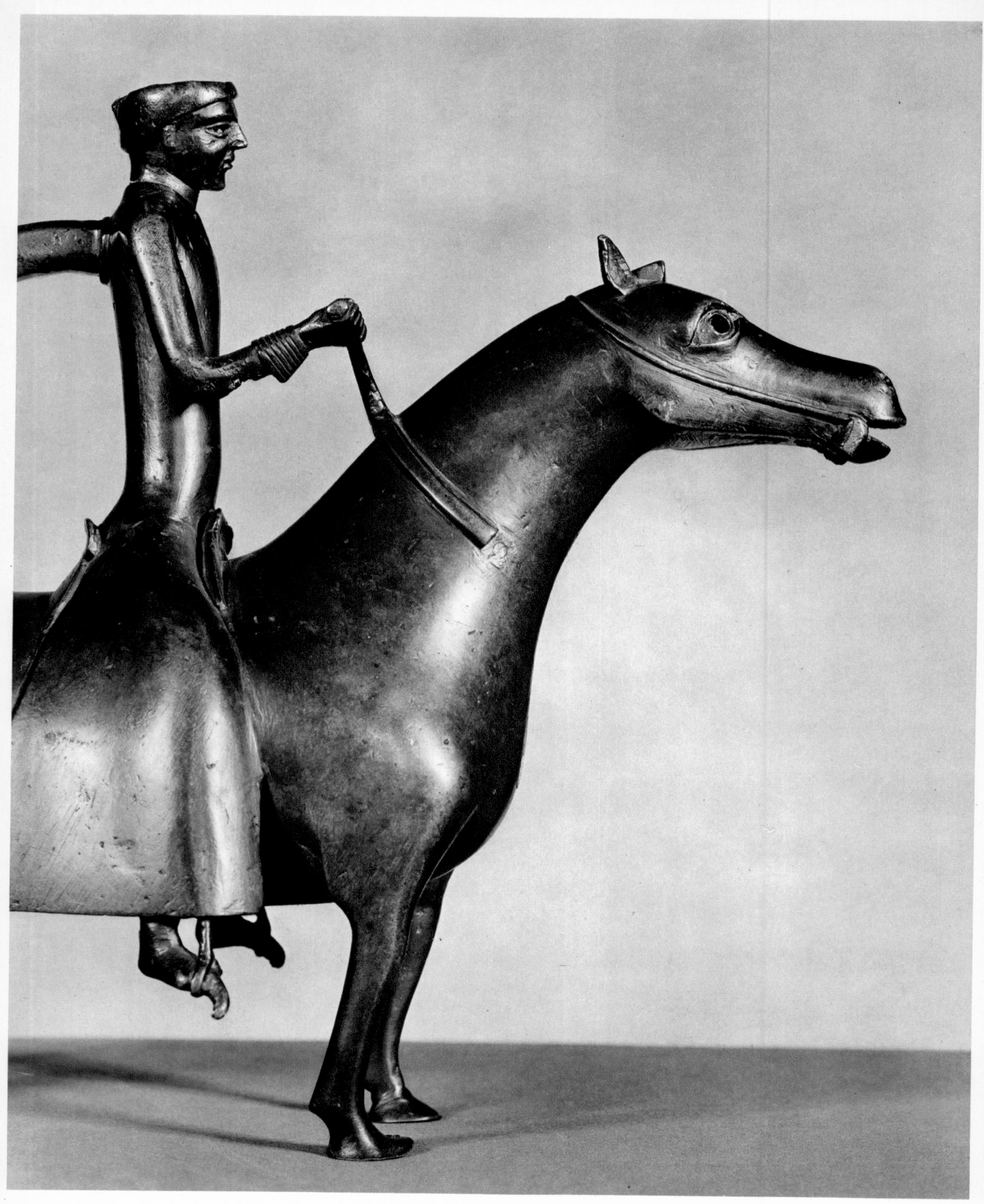

ENGLISH(?), XIII CENTURY · *Horseman, Aquamanile,* Detail. See Page 33

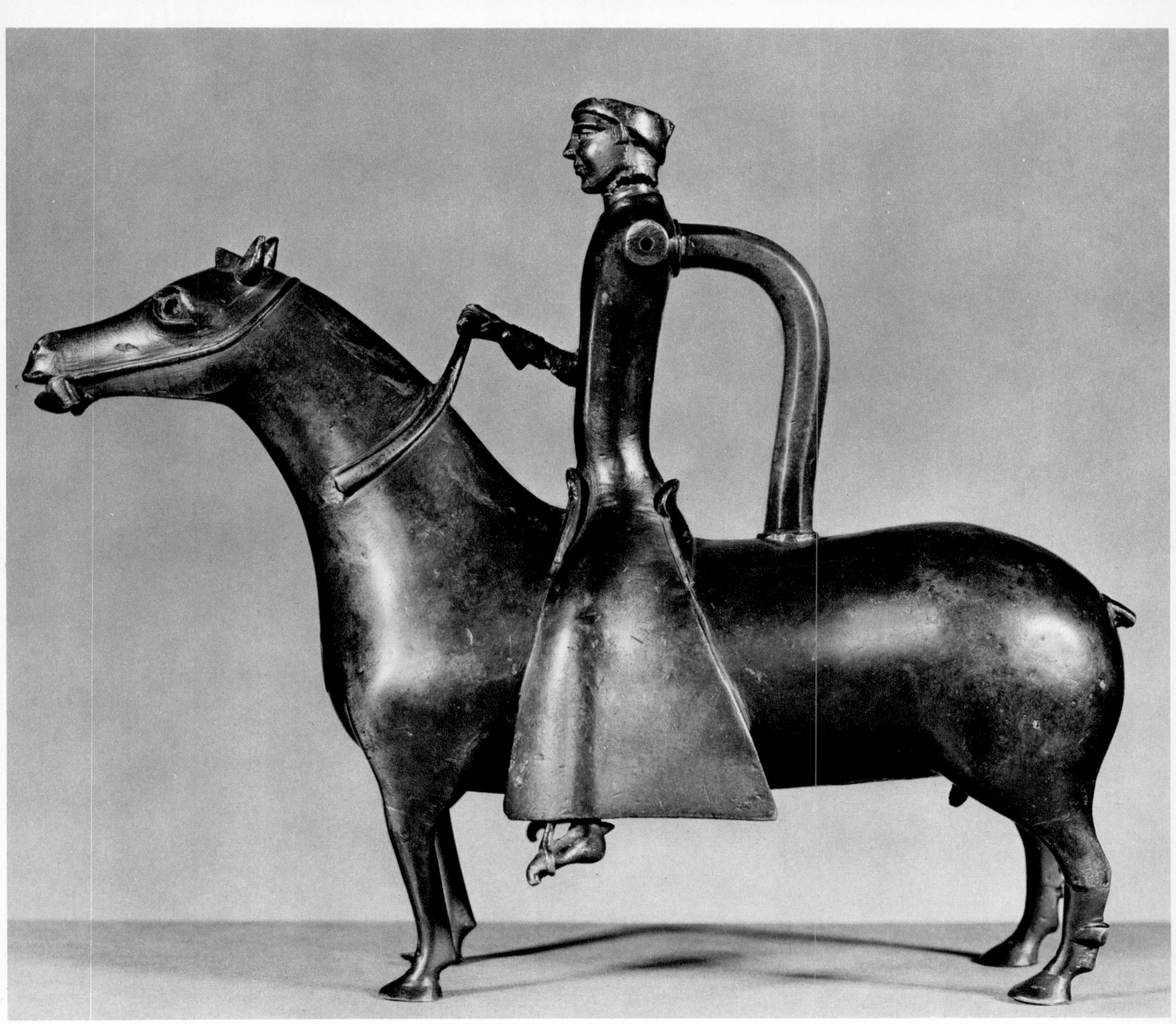

Bronze H. $11\frac{3}{16}$ in.

ENGLISH(?), XIII CENTURY · *Horseman, Aquamanile.* *Widener Collection.* See Note 4

34016

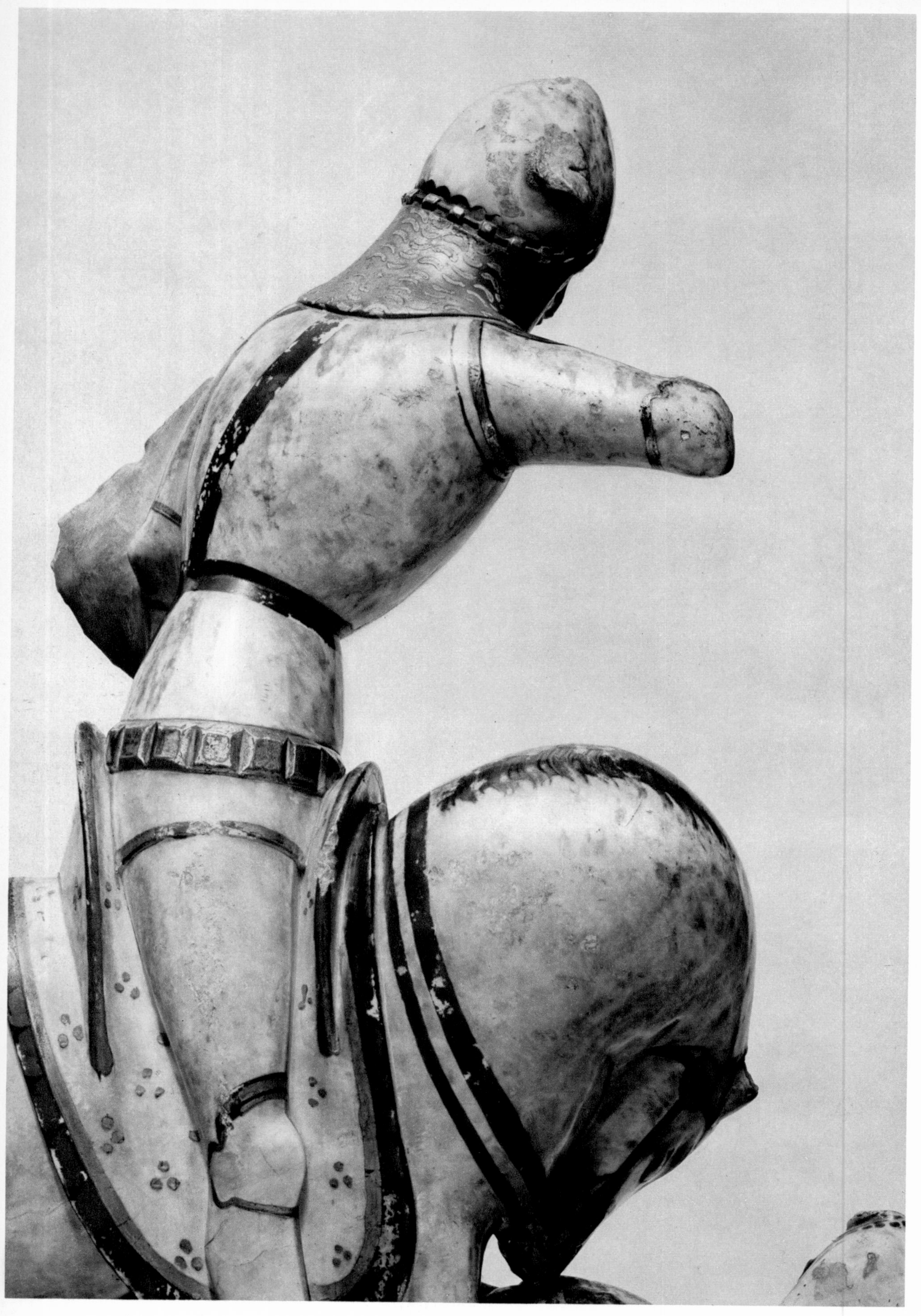

ENGLISH, LATE XIV OR EARLY XV CENTURY · *Saint George and the Dragon,* Detail. See Page 36

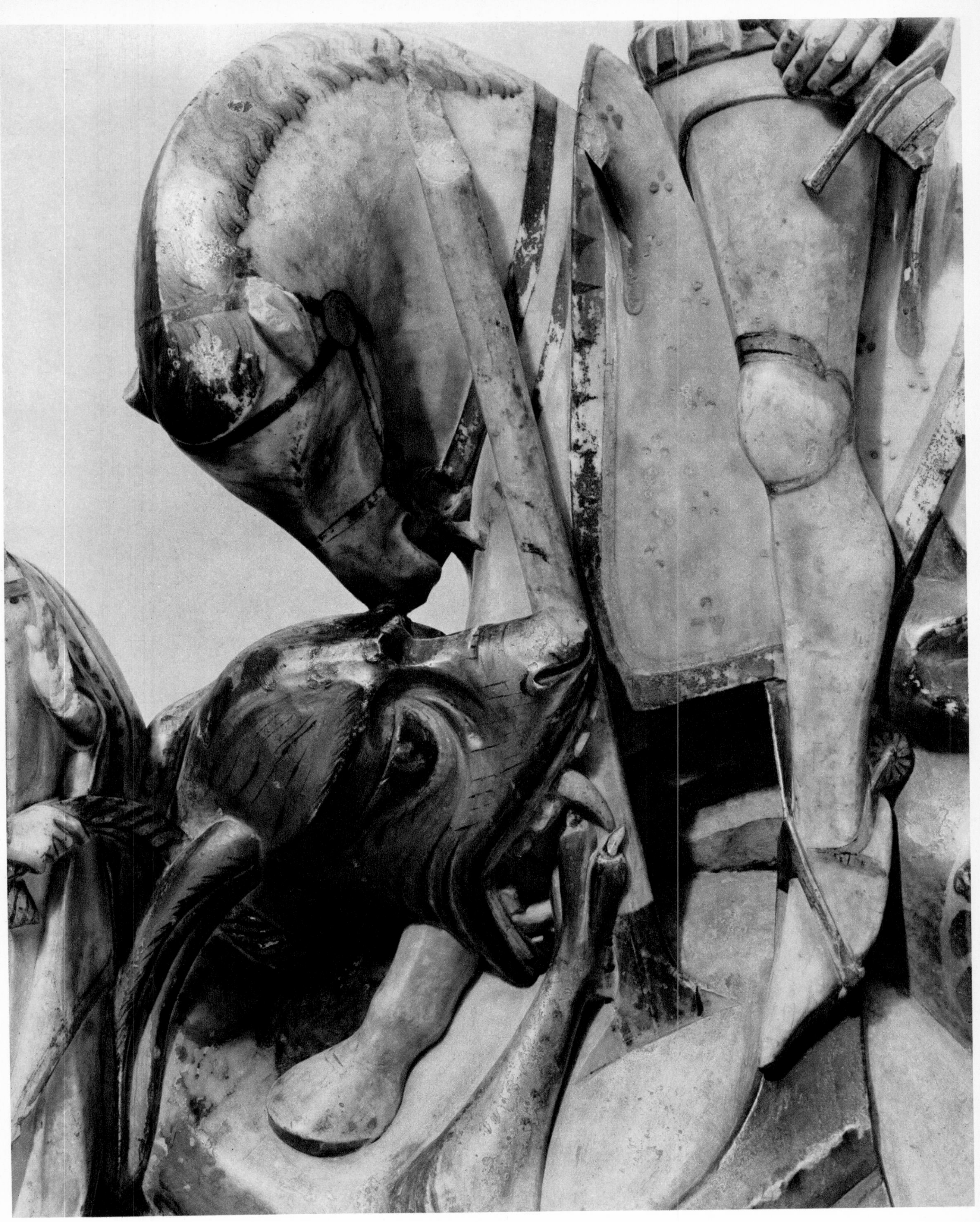

ENGLISH, LATE XIV OR EARLY XV CENTURY · *Saint George and the Dragon,* Detail. See Page 36

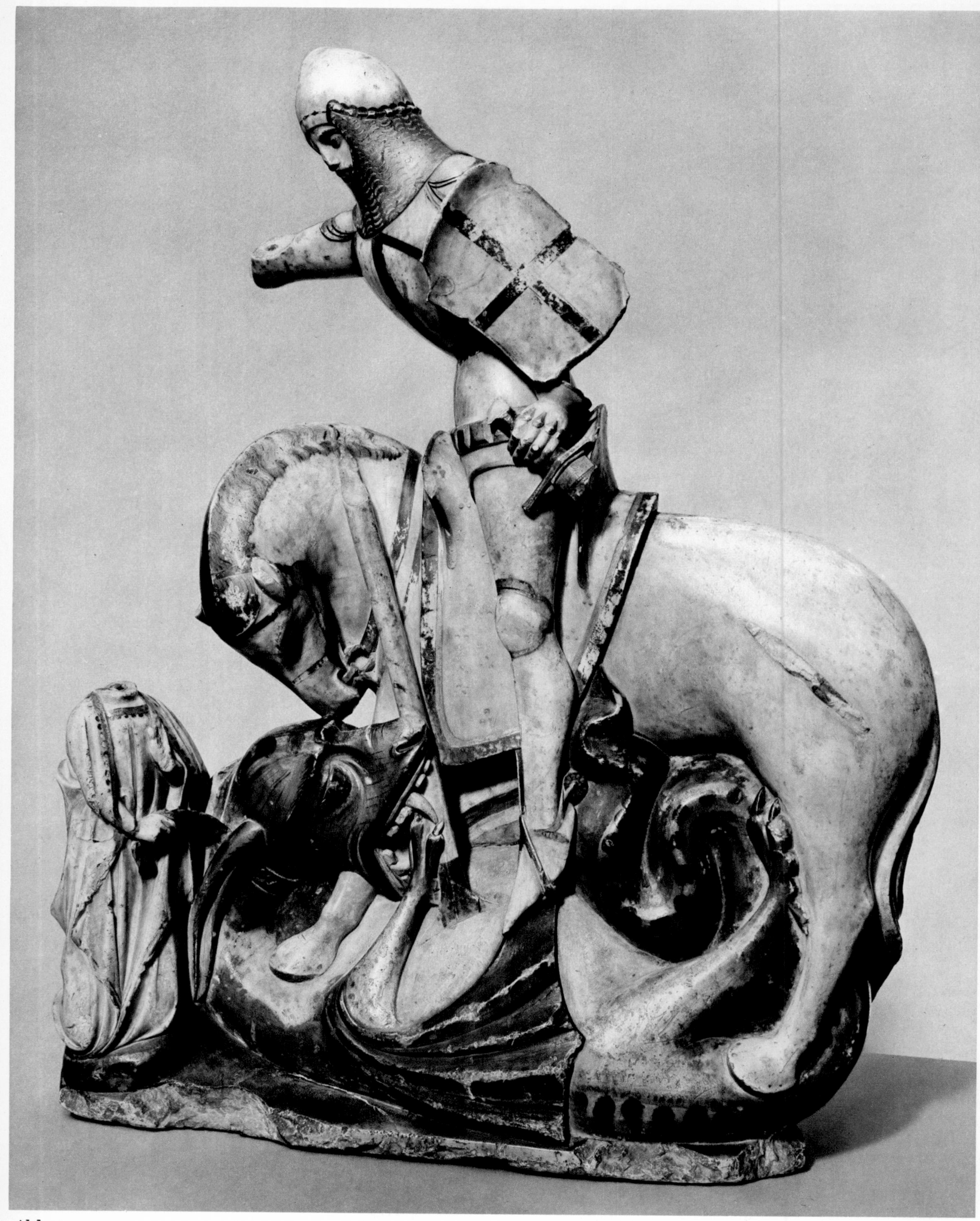

Alabaster H. $31^{31}/_{32}$ in.

ENGLISH, LATE XIV OR EARLY XV CENTURY · *Saint George and the Dragon.* *Kress Collection.* See Note 5

Bronze

Enlarged

PISANELLO · *Medal of Domenico Malatesta,* Reverse. *Kress Collection, Loan.* See Note 6

Bronze Enlarged

BURGUNDIAN, XIV CENTURY · *Medal of Heraclius.* *Kress Collection, Loan.* See Notes 7, 8

Bronze　　　　Enlarged

BURGUNDIAN, XIV CENTURY · *Medal of Constantine.* *Kress Collection, Loan.* See Notes 7, 8

FRENCH OR BURGUNDIAN, c. 1400 · *The Trinity,* Detail. See Page 41

Gold and enamel — Diam. 5 in.

FRENCH OR BURGUNDIAN, c. 1400 · *The Trinity.* *Widener Collection.* See Note 9

FRENCH OR BURGUNDIAN, c. 1400 · *The Trinity,* Detail. See Page 41

ENGLISH, XIV CENTURY · *The Holy Trinity,* Detail. See Page 45

ENGLISH, XIV CENTURY · *The Holy Trinity*, Detail. See Page 45

Alabaster

H. $33^{19}/_{32}$ in.

ENGLISH, XIV CENTURY · *The Holy Trinity.* *Kress Collection.* See Note 10

UPPER RHENISH, EARLY XV CENTURY · *The Dead Christ Supported by an Angel,* Detail. See Page 48

UPPER RHENISH, EARLY XV CENTURY · *The Dead Christ Supported by an Angel,* Detail. See Page 48

Painted Alabaster

H. 12¼ in.

UPPER RHENISH, EARLY XV CENTURY · *The Dead Christ Supported by an Angel.* *Booth Collection.* See Note 11

Alabaster H. 20¼ in.

TINO DI CAMAINO · *Madonna and Child with Queen Sancia, Saints and Angels.* *Kress Collection.* See Note 12

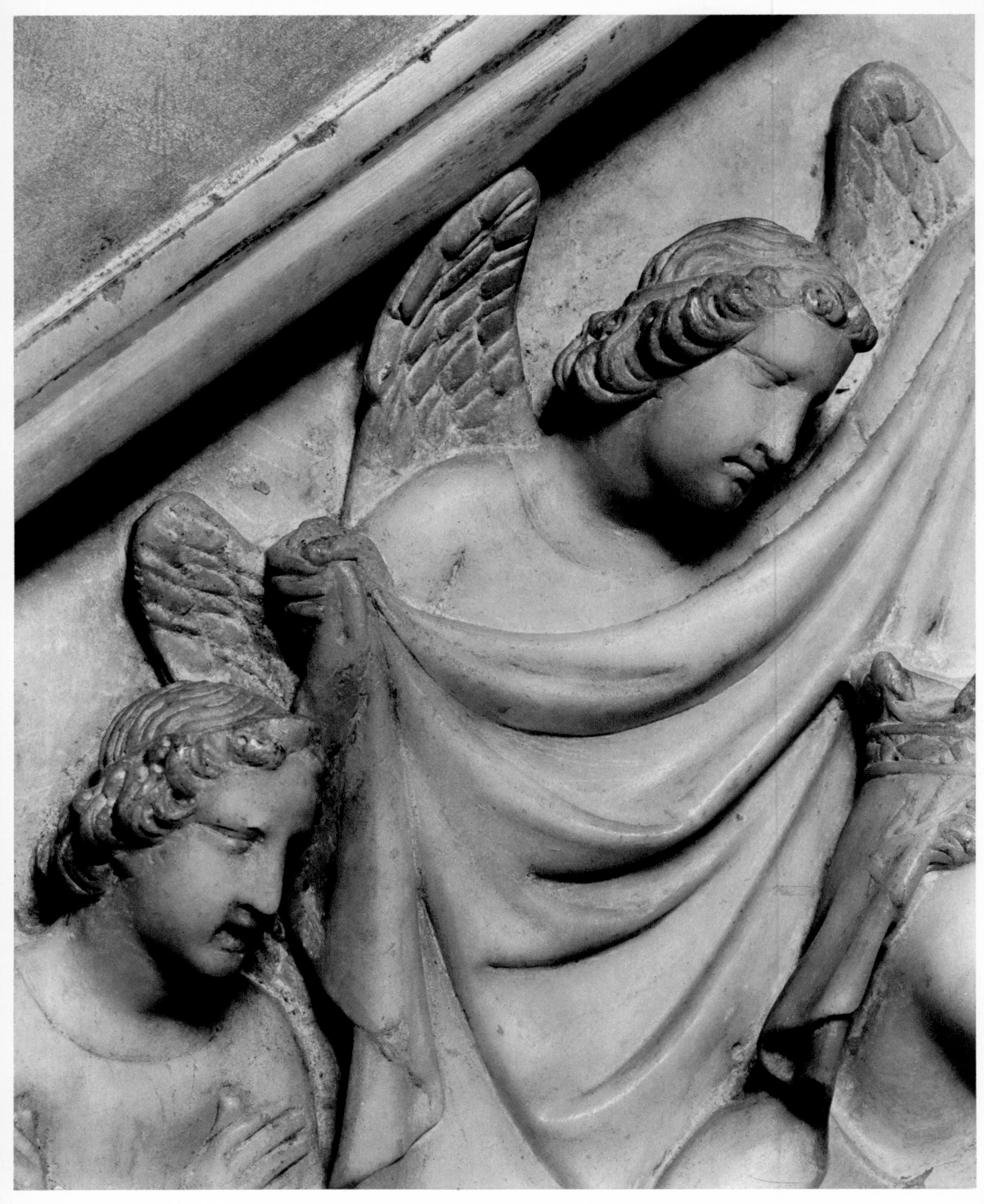

TINO DI CAMAINO · *Madonna and Child with Queen Sancia, Saints and Angels,* Detail. See Page 49

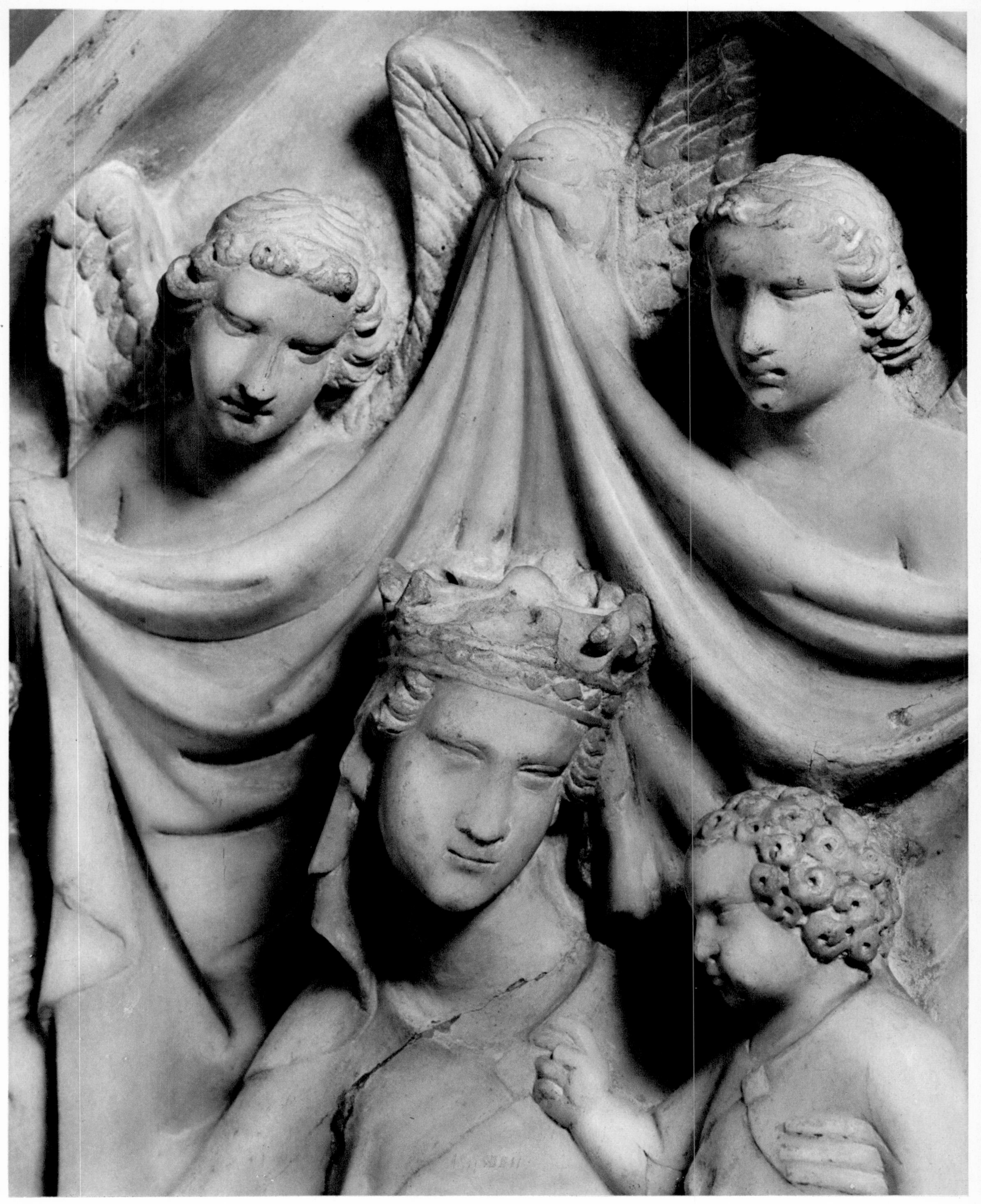

TINO DI CAMAINO · *Madonna and Child with Queen Sancia, Saints and Angels,* Detail. See Page 49

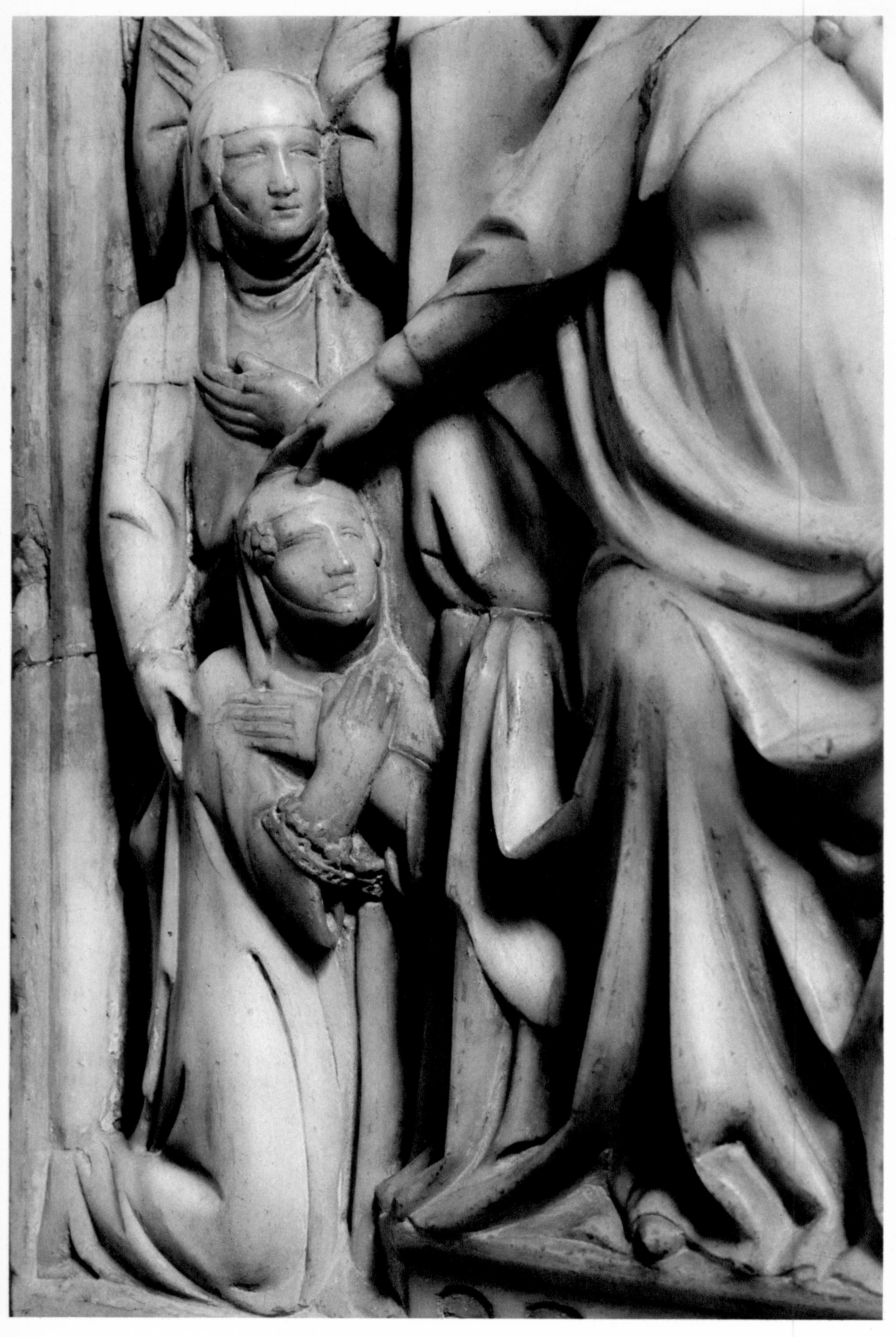

TINO DI CAMAINO · *Madonna and Child with Queen Sancia, Saints and Angels,* Detail. See Page 49

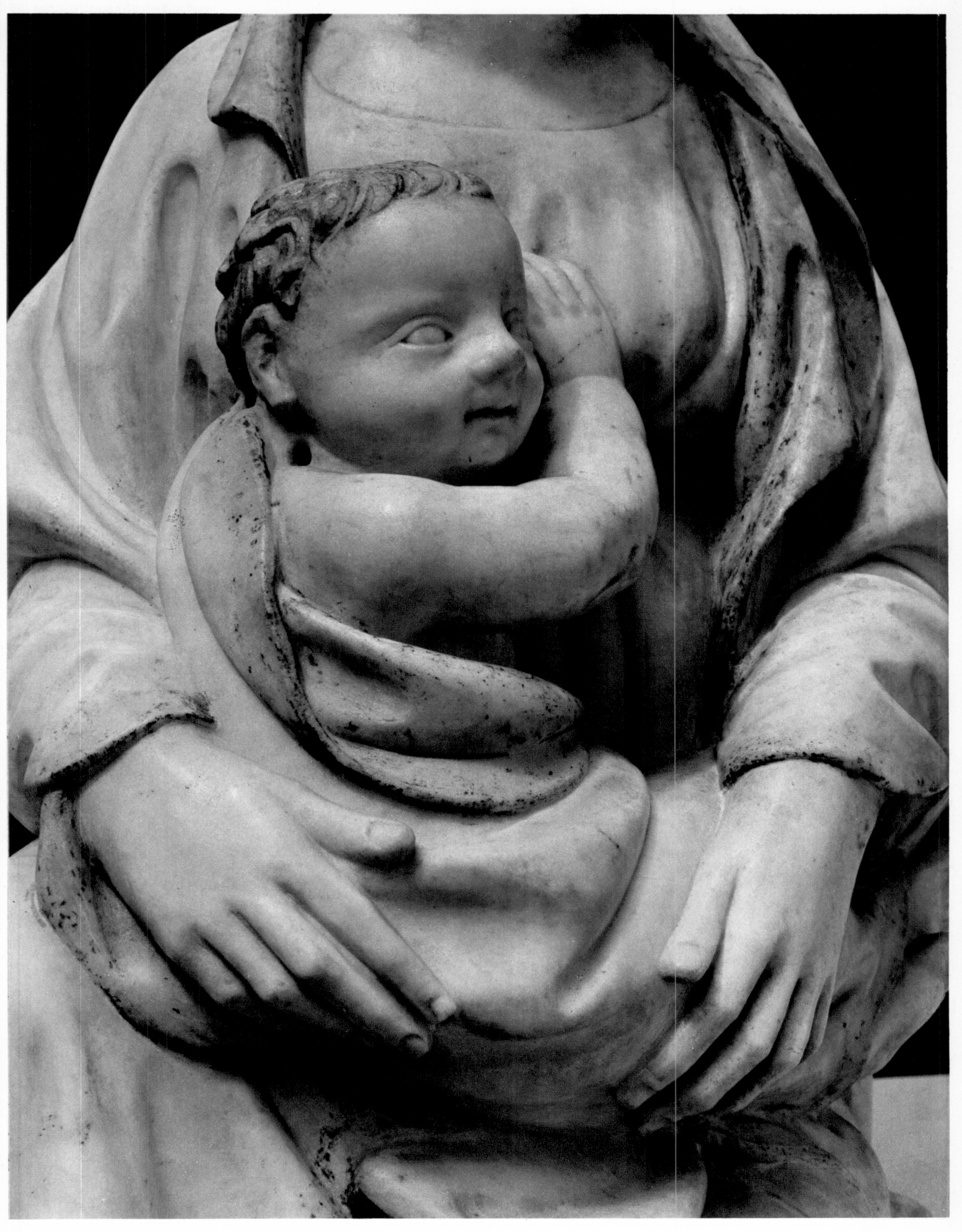

JACOPO DELLA QUERCIA · *Madonna of Humility*, Detail. See Page 54

Marble, with traces of gilt H. 22 31/32 in.

JACOPO DELLA QUERCIA · *Madonna of Humility.* *Kress Collection.* See Note 13

JACOPO DELLA QUERCIA · *Madonna of Humility*, Detail. See Page 54

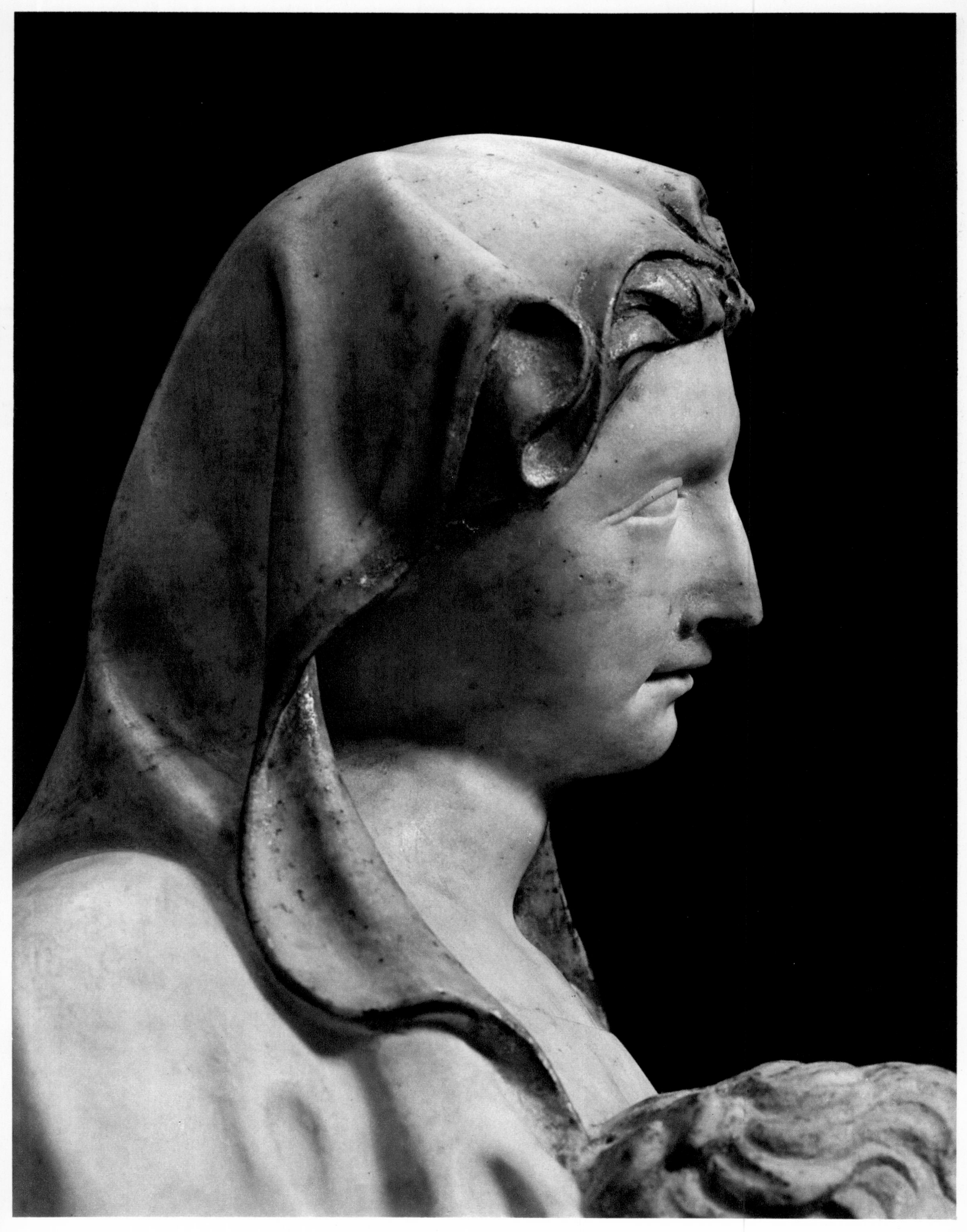

JACOPO DELLA QUERCIA · *Madonna of Humility,* Detail. See Page 54

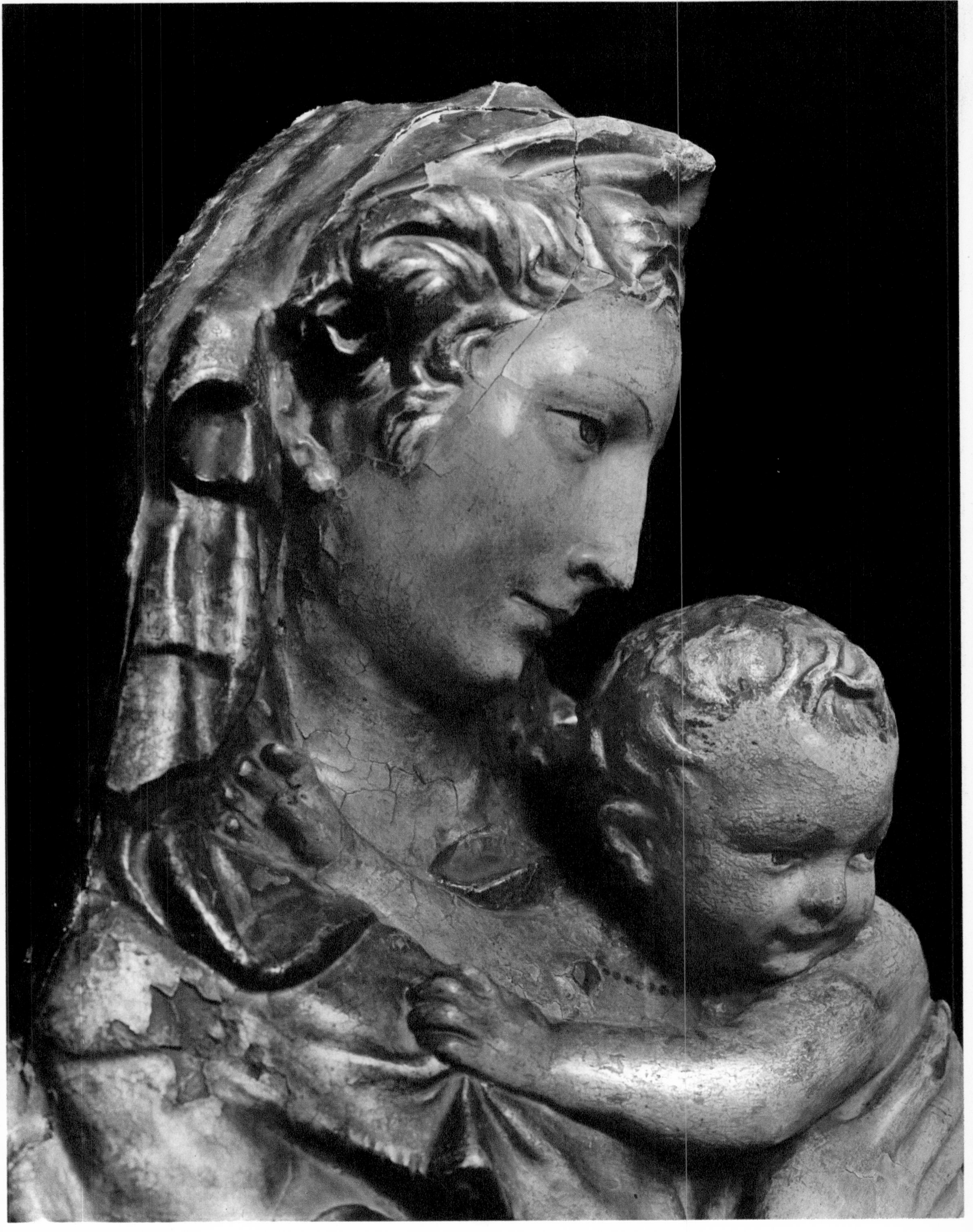

LORENZO GHIBERTI · *Madonna and Child,* Detail. See Page 58

Painted terra cotta H. 40⅜ in.

LORENZO GHIBERTI · *Madonna and Child.* *Kress Collection.* See Note 14

Painted terra cotta H. 47 9/16 in.

DONATELLO · *Madonna and Child.* Mellon Collection. See Note 15

LORENZO GHIBERTI · *Madonna and Child,* Detail. See Page 58

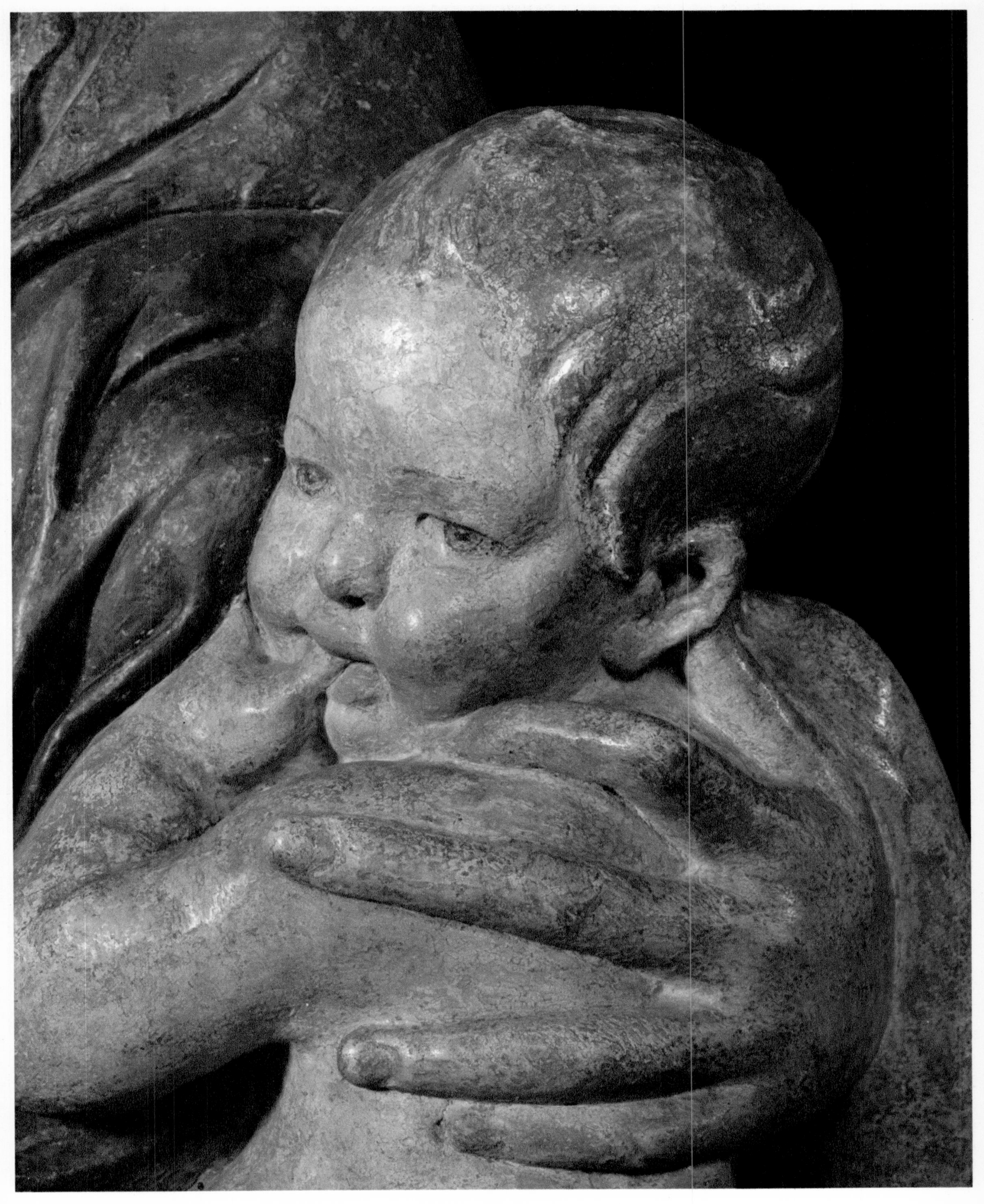

DONATELLO · *Madonna and Child,* Detail. See Page 59

DONATELLO · *Madonna and Child,* Detail. See Page 59

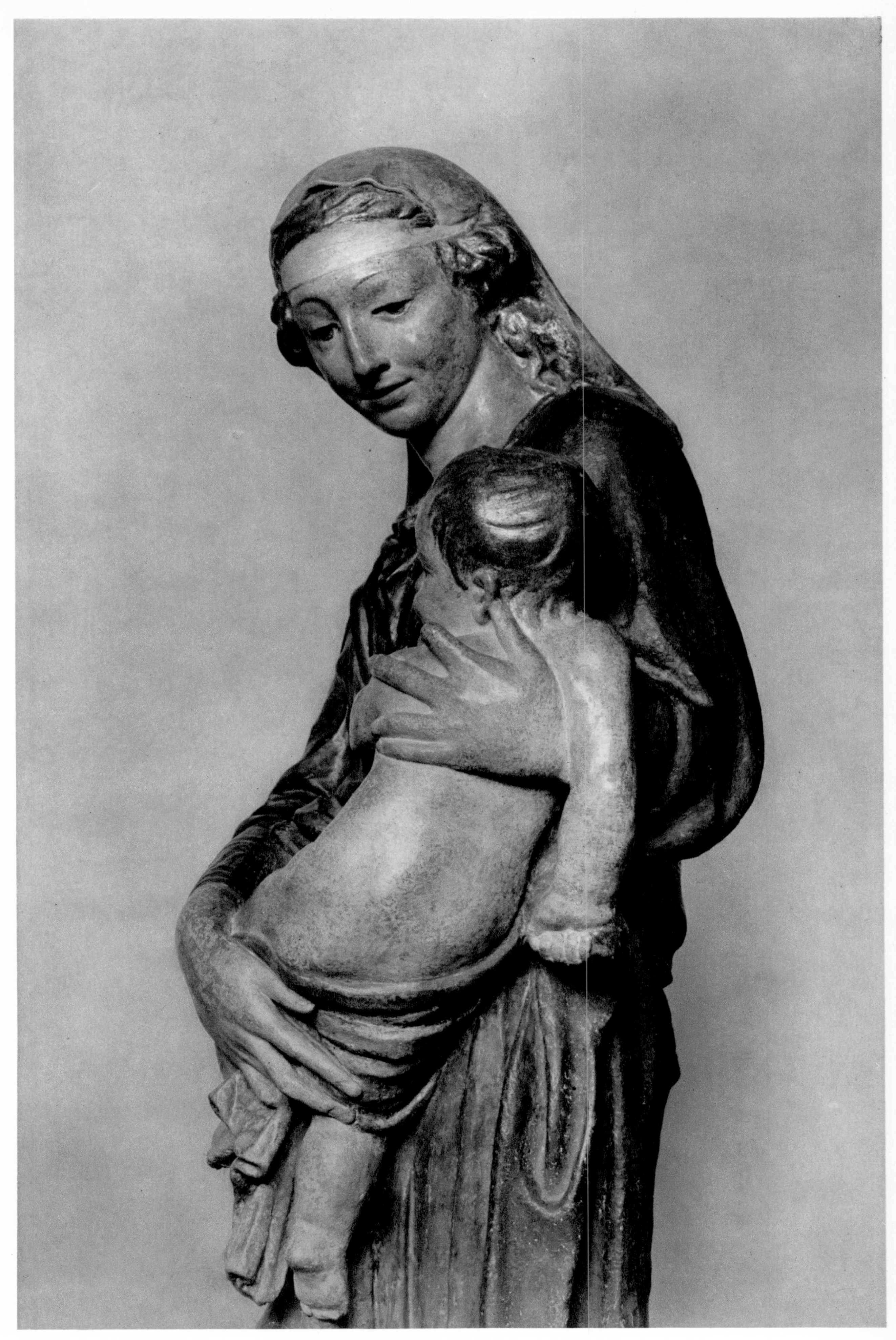

DONATELLO · *Madonna and Child,* Detail. See Page 59

Glazed terra cotta H. 24⅜ in.

MICHELOZZO · *Madonna with the Sleeping Child.* *Kress Collection.* See Note 16

MICHELOZZO · *Madonna with the Sleeping Child,* Detail. See Page 64

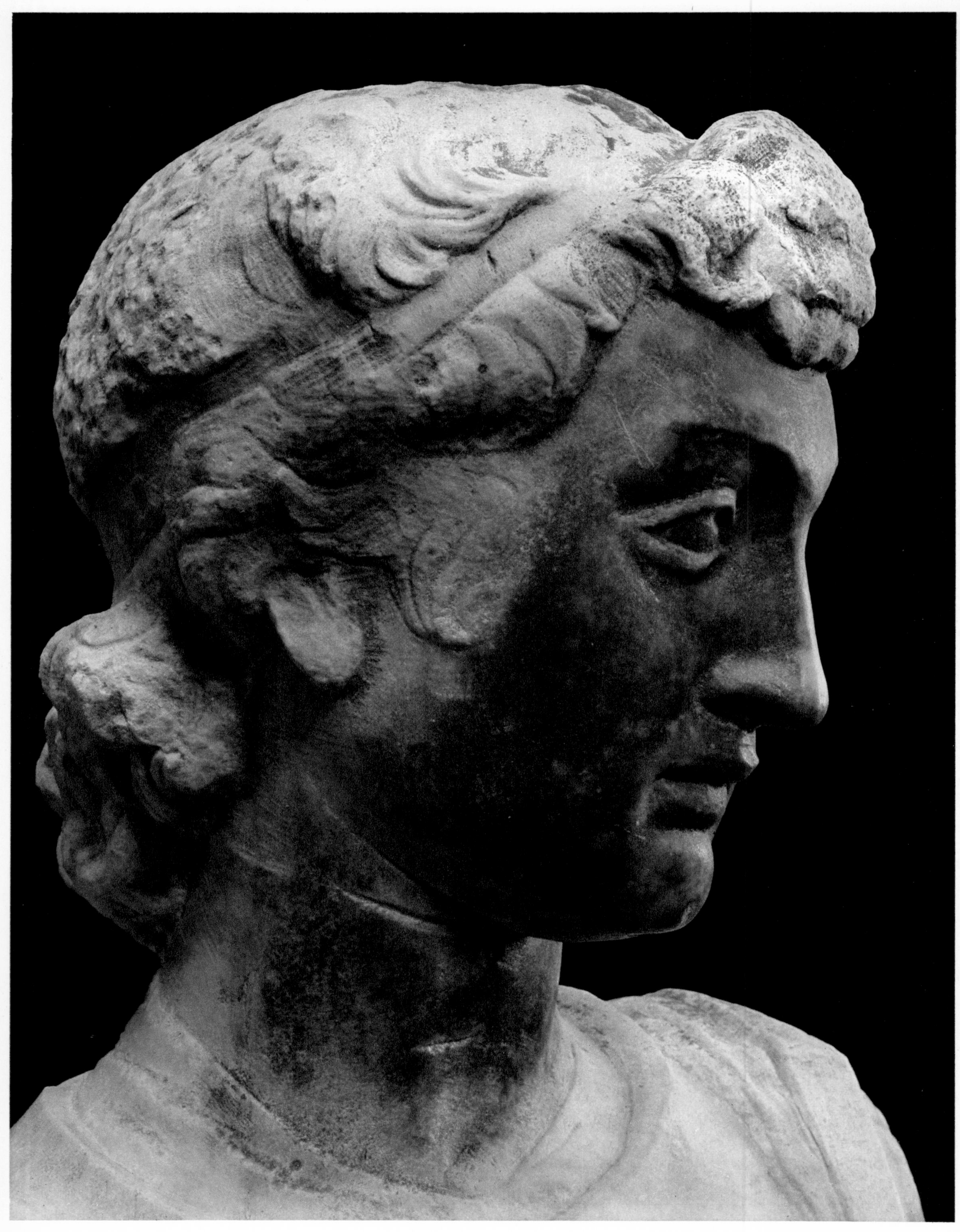

DONATELLO · *David of the Casa Martelli,* Detail. See Page 67

Marble H. 64 in.

DONATELLO · *David of the Casa Martelli.* *Widener Collection.* See Note 17

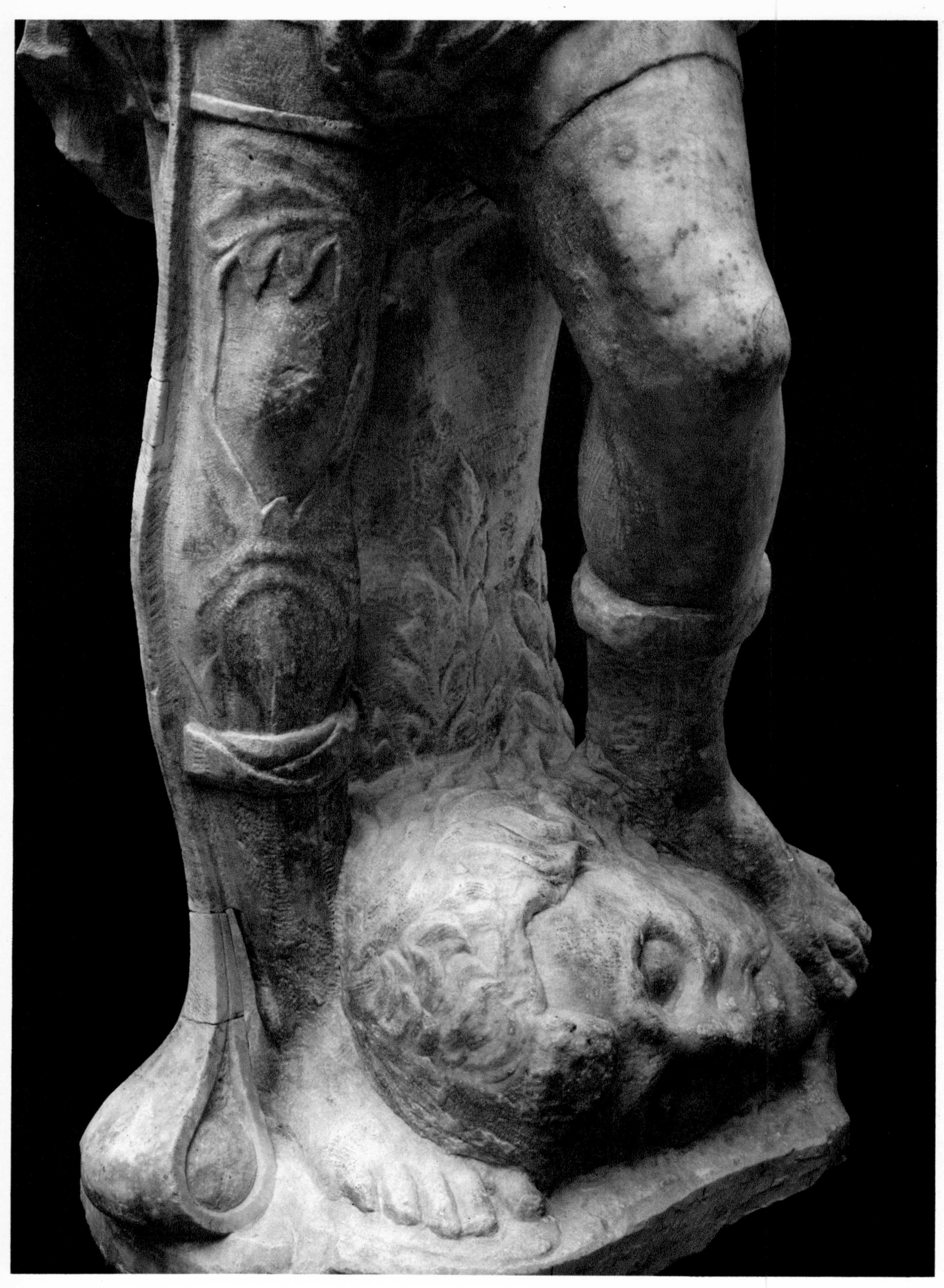

DONATELLO · *David of the Casa Martelli,* Detail. See Page 67

DONATELLO · *David of the Casa Martelli,* Detail. See Page 67

DONATELLO · *David of the Casa Martelli,* Detail. See Page 67

DONATELLO · *David of the Casa Martelli,* Detail. See Page 67

Painted terra cotta H. 19¼ in.

DONATELLO · *Saint John the Baptist.* *Mellon Collection.* See Note 18

DONATELLO · *Saint John the Baptist,* Detail. See Page 72

Marble H. 12 in.

DESIDERIO DA SETTIGNANO · *The Christ Child.* *Kress Collection.* See Note 19

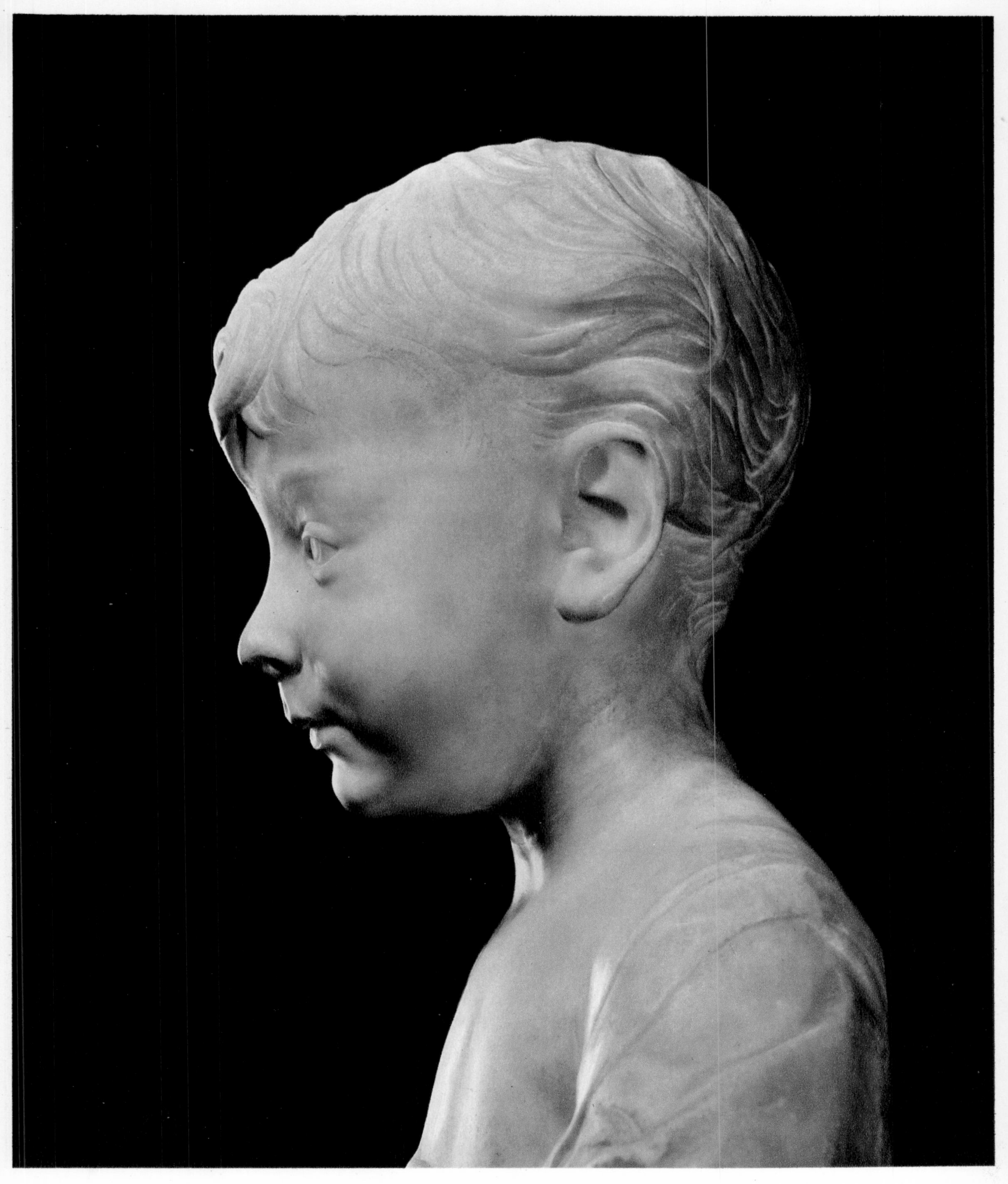

DESIDERIO DA SETTIGNANO · *The Christ Child*, **Detail.** See Page 74

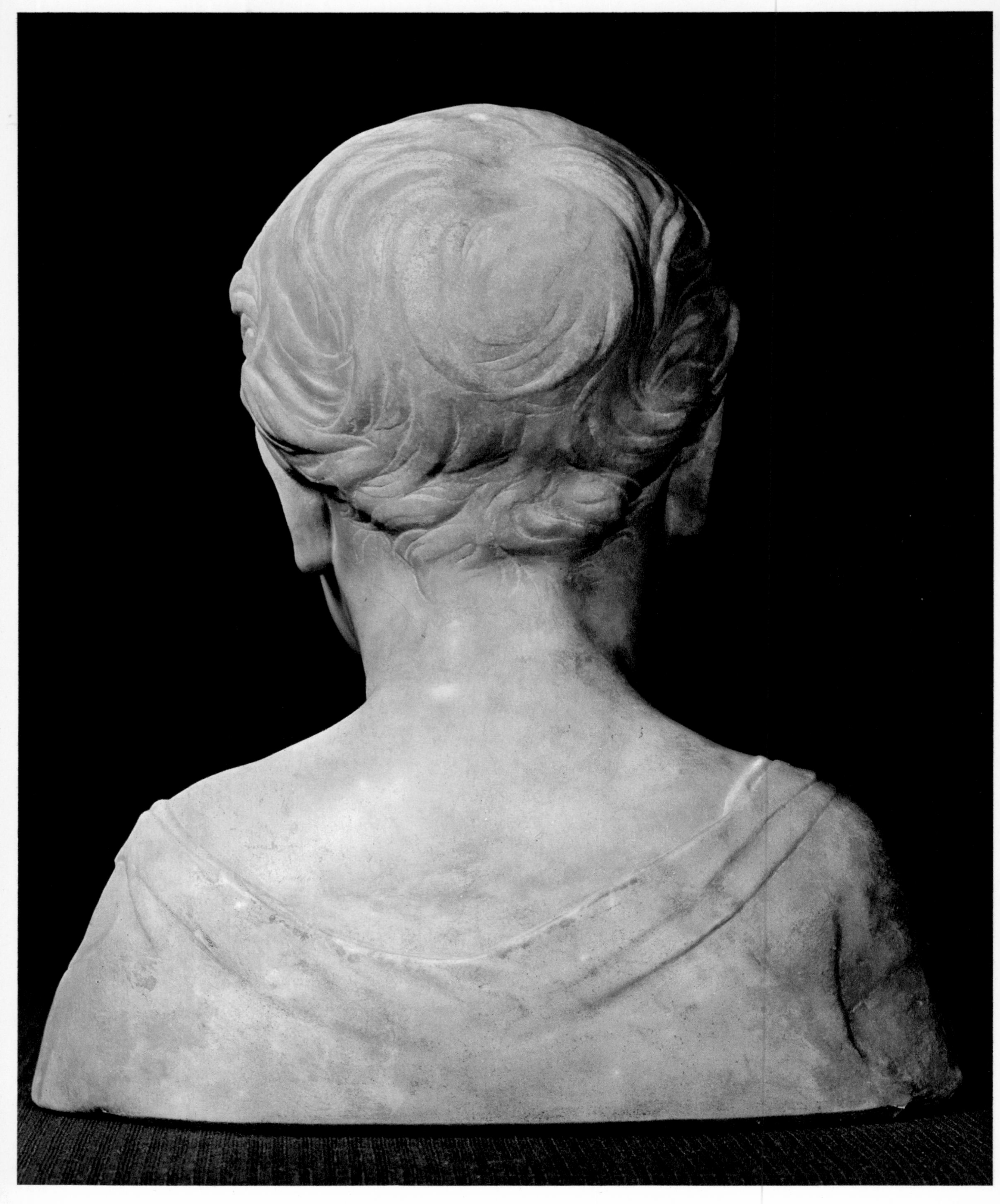

DESIDERIO DA SETTIGNANO · *The Christ Child,* Rear View. See Page 74

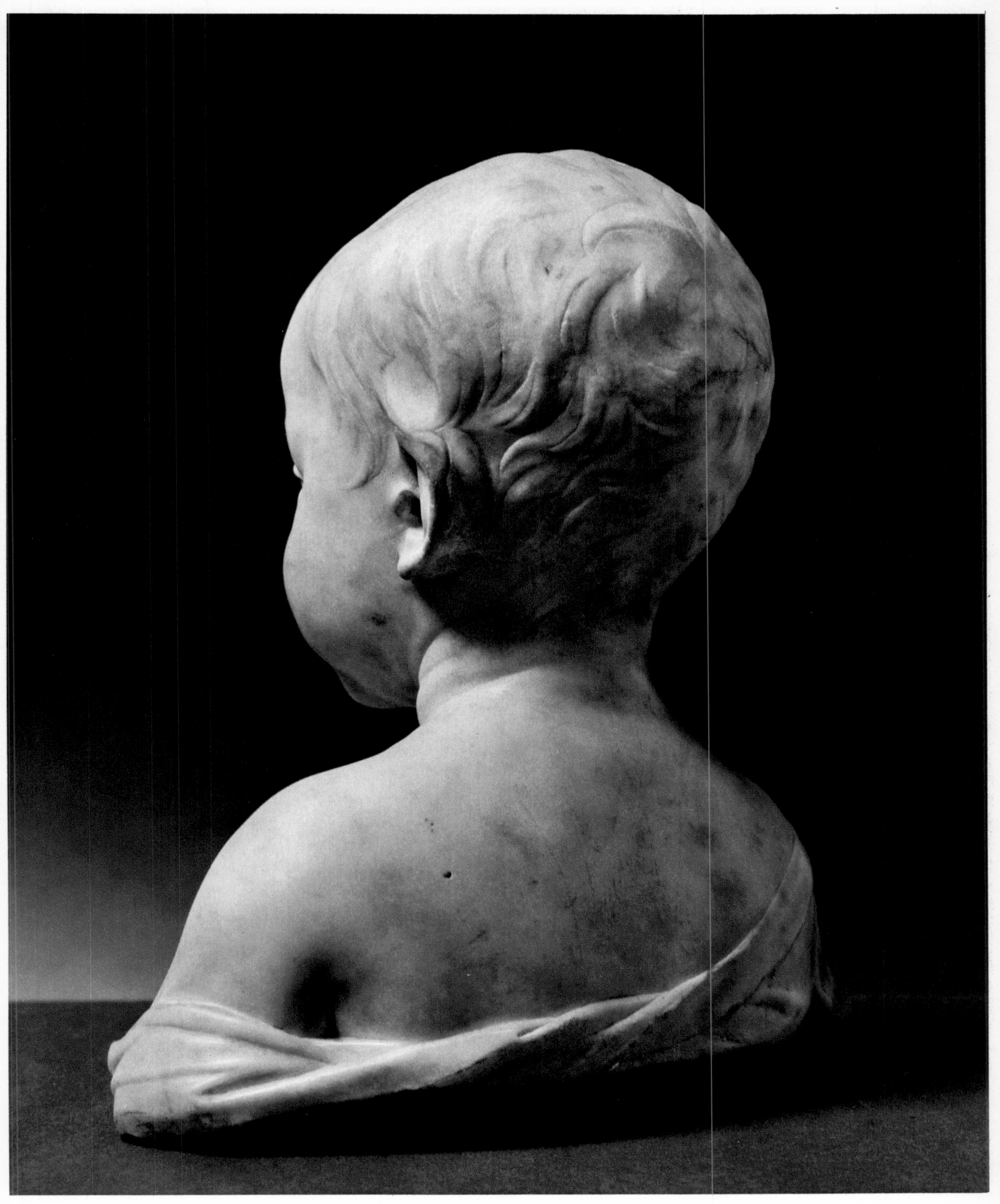

DESIDERIO DA SETTIGNANO · *Bust of a Little Boy,* Rear View. See Page 79

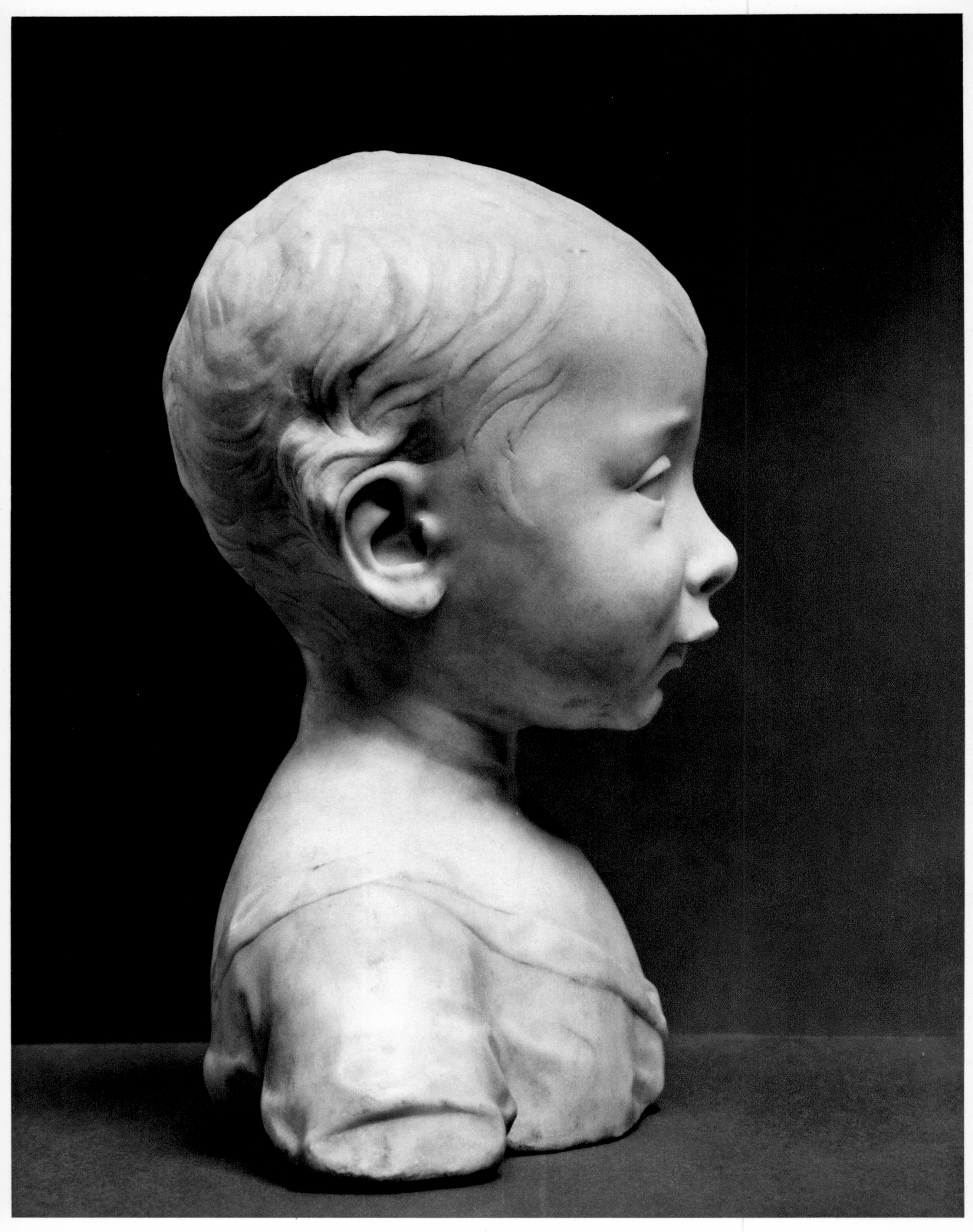

DESIDERIO DA SETTIGNANO · *Bust of a Little Boy,* Side View. See Page 79

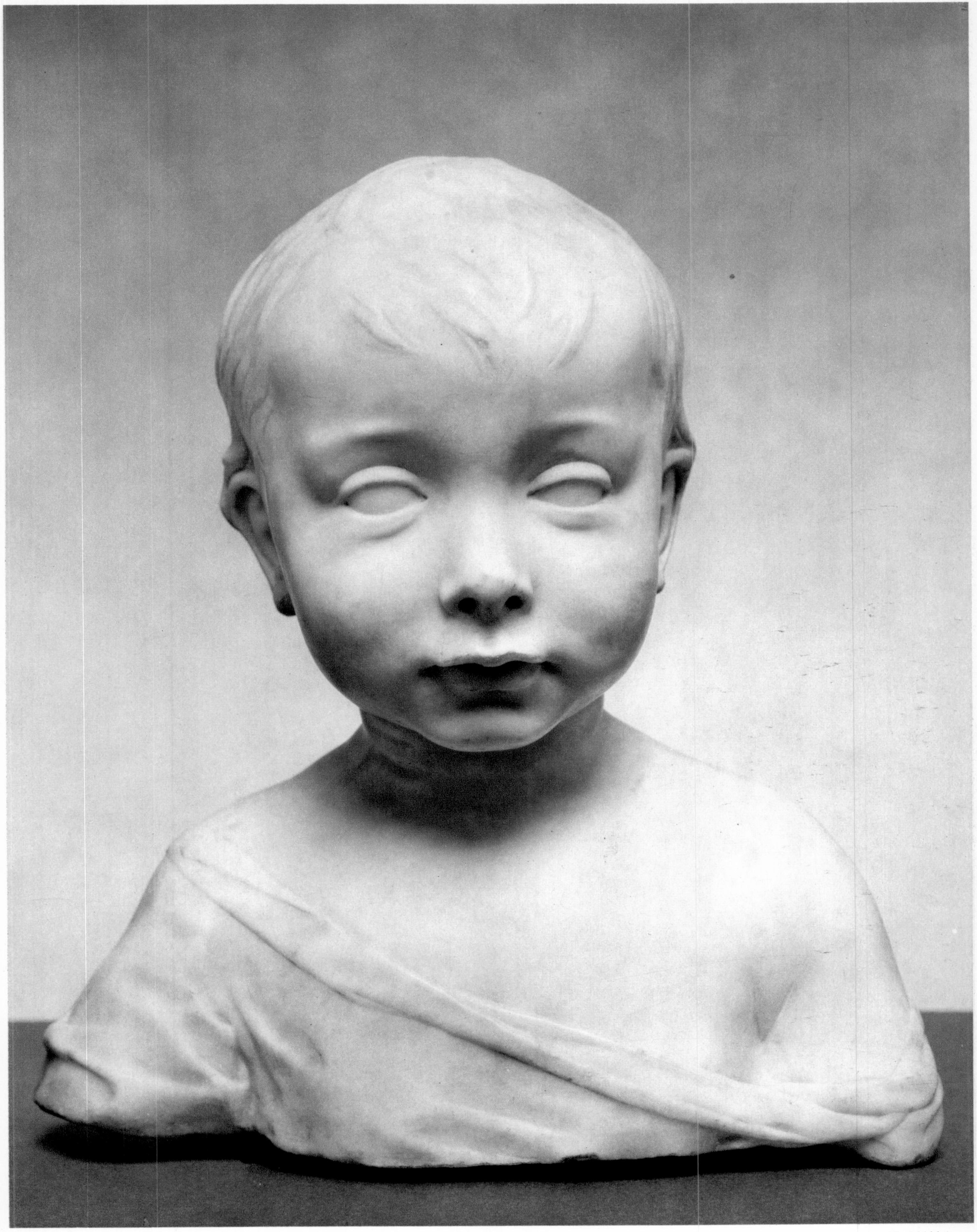

Marble H. $10^{11}/_{32}$ in.

DESIDERIO DA SETTIGNANO · *Bust of a Little Boy.* *Mellon Collection.* See Note 20

Marble

H. 13⅝ in.

ANTONIO ROSSELLINO · *The Young Saint John the Baptist.* *Kress Collection.* See Note 21

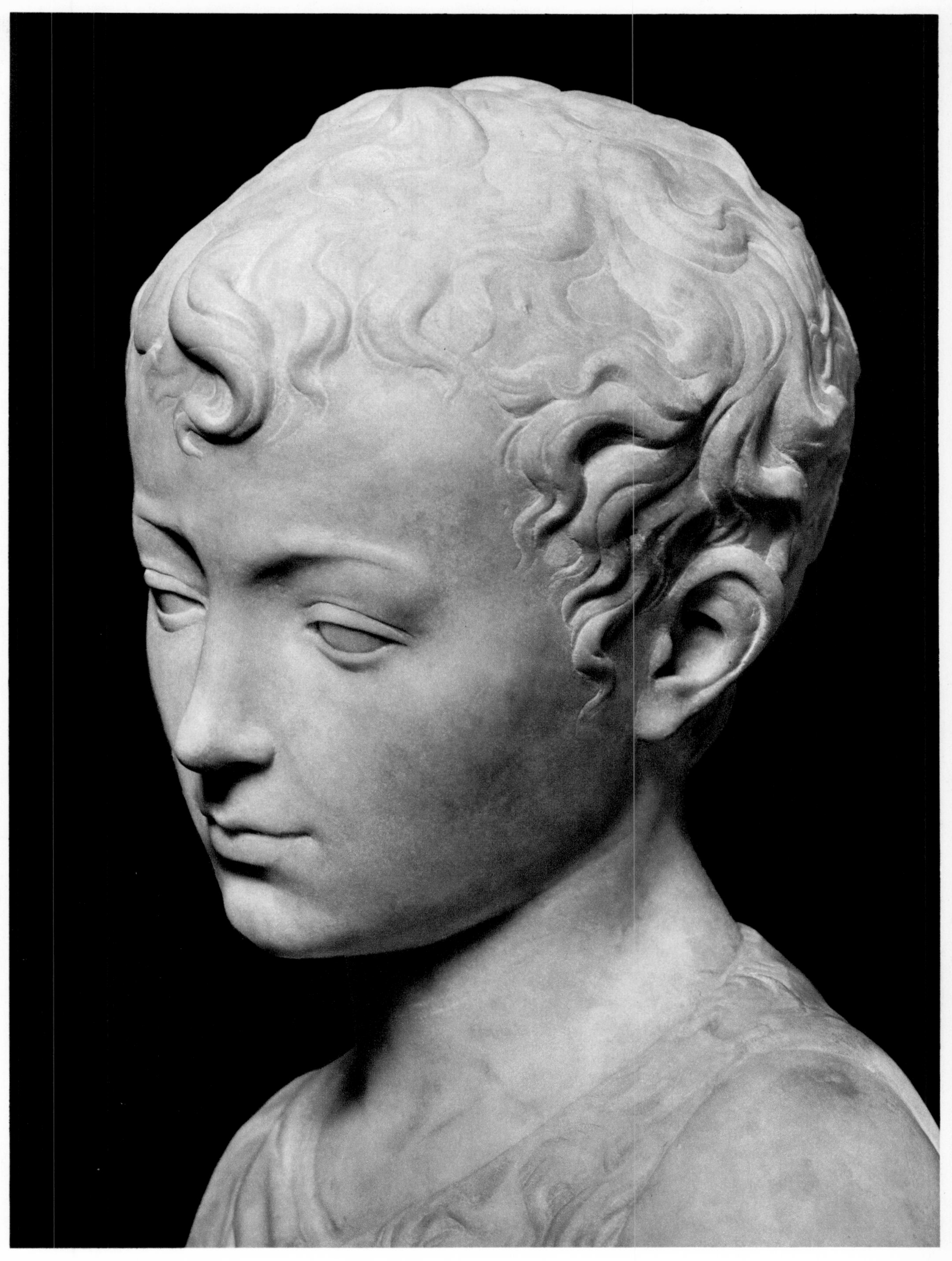

ANTONIO ROSSELLINO · *The Young Saint John the Baptist,* Detail. See Page 80

DESIDERIO DA SETTIGNANO · *Marietta Strozzi,* Detail. See Page 83

Marble H. 22⅛ in.

DESIDERIO DA SETTIGNANO · *Marietta Strozzi.* *Widener Collection.* See Note 22

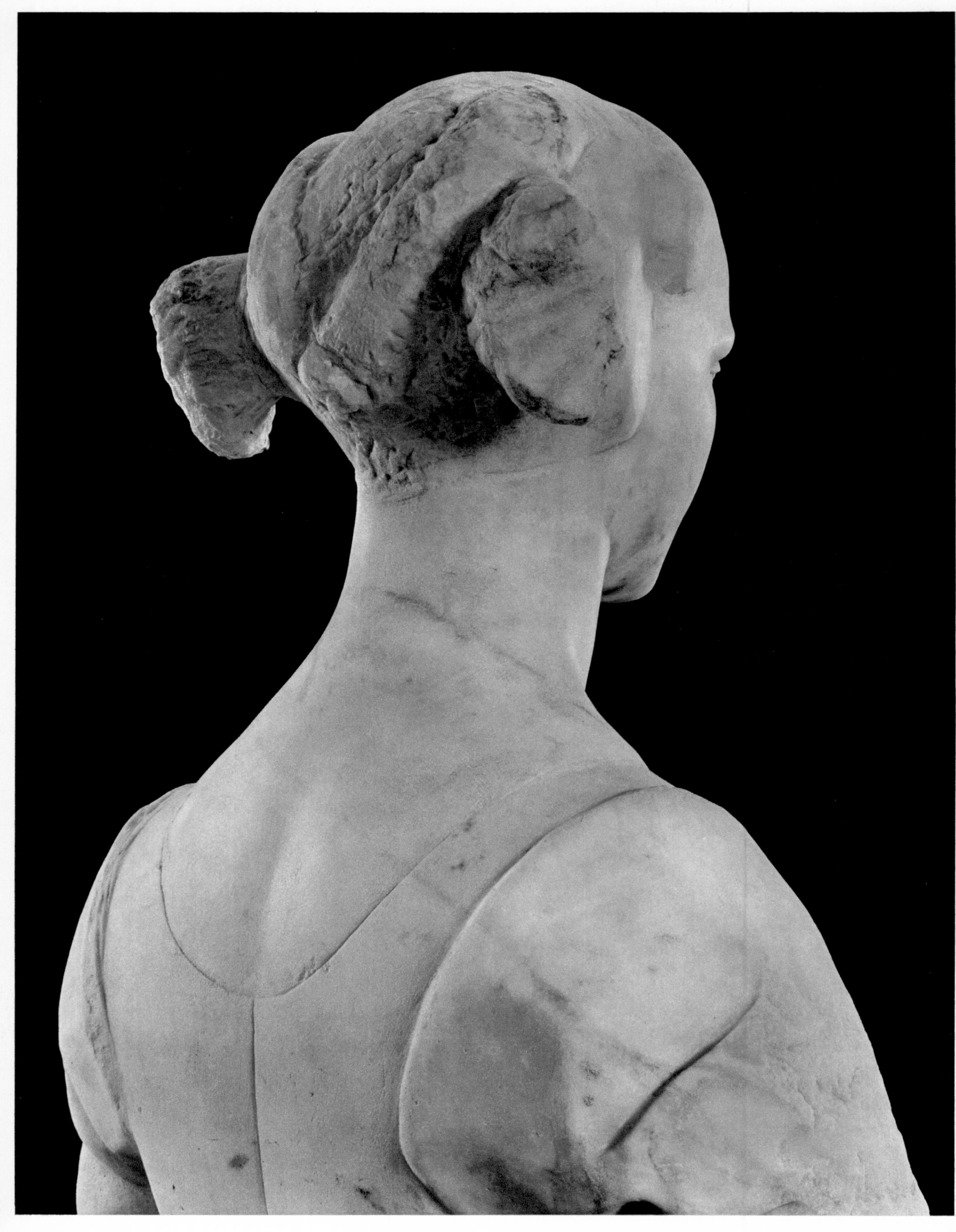

DESIDERIO DA SETTIGNANO · *Marietta Strozzi,* Detail. See Page 83

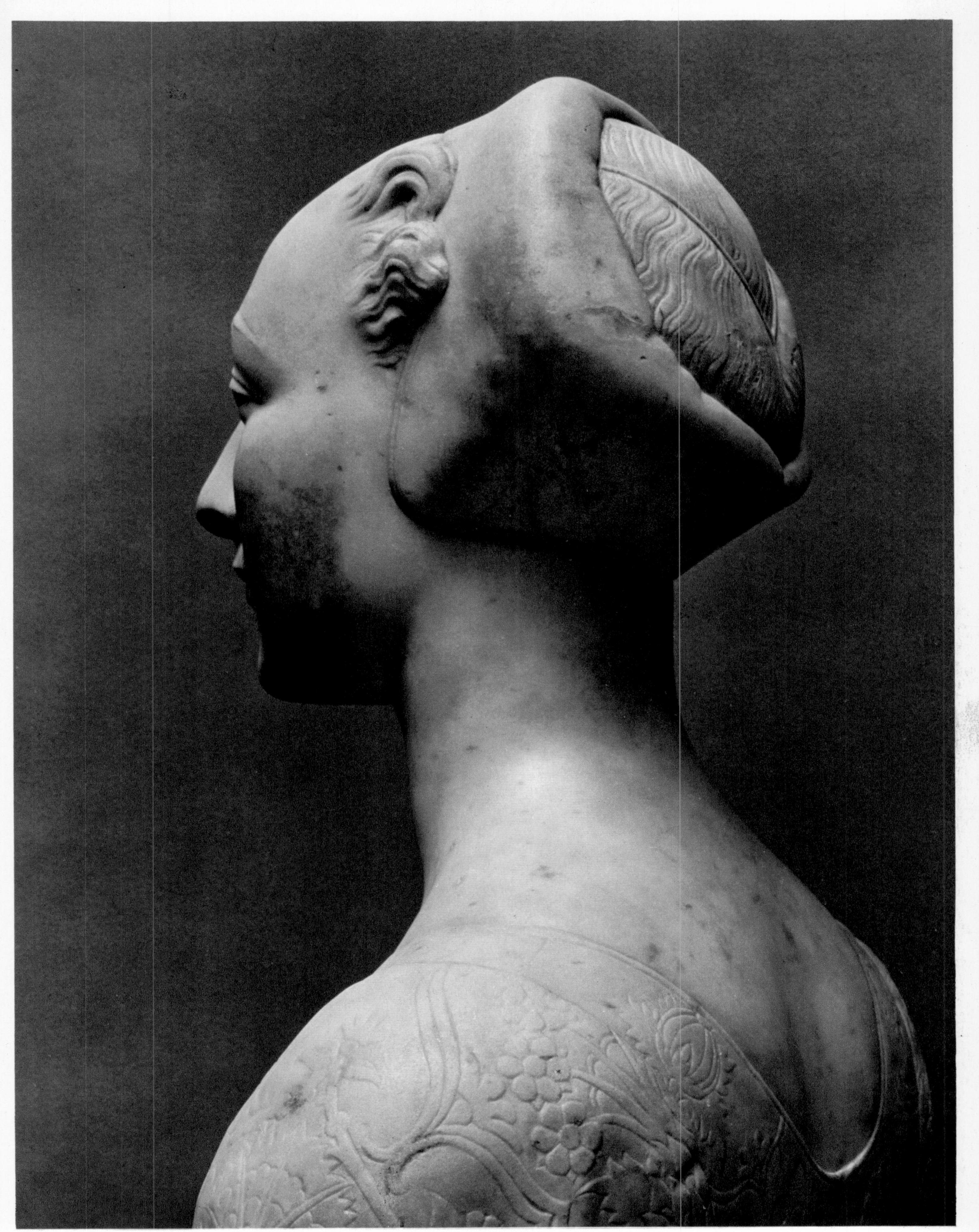

DESIDERIO DA SETTIGNANO · *Bust of a Lady,* Detail. See Page 86

Marble H. 20⅞ in.

DESIDERIO DA SETTIGNANO · *Bust of a Lady.* *Kress Collection.* See Note 23

Marble

H. 17 15/32 in.

FRANCESCO DA LAURANA · *A Princess of the House of Aragon.* *Mellon Collection.* See Note 24

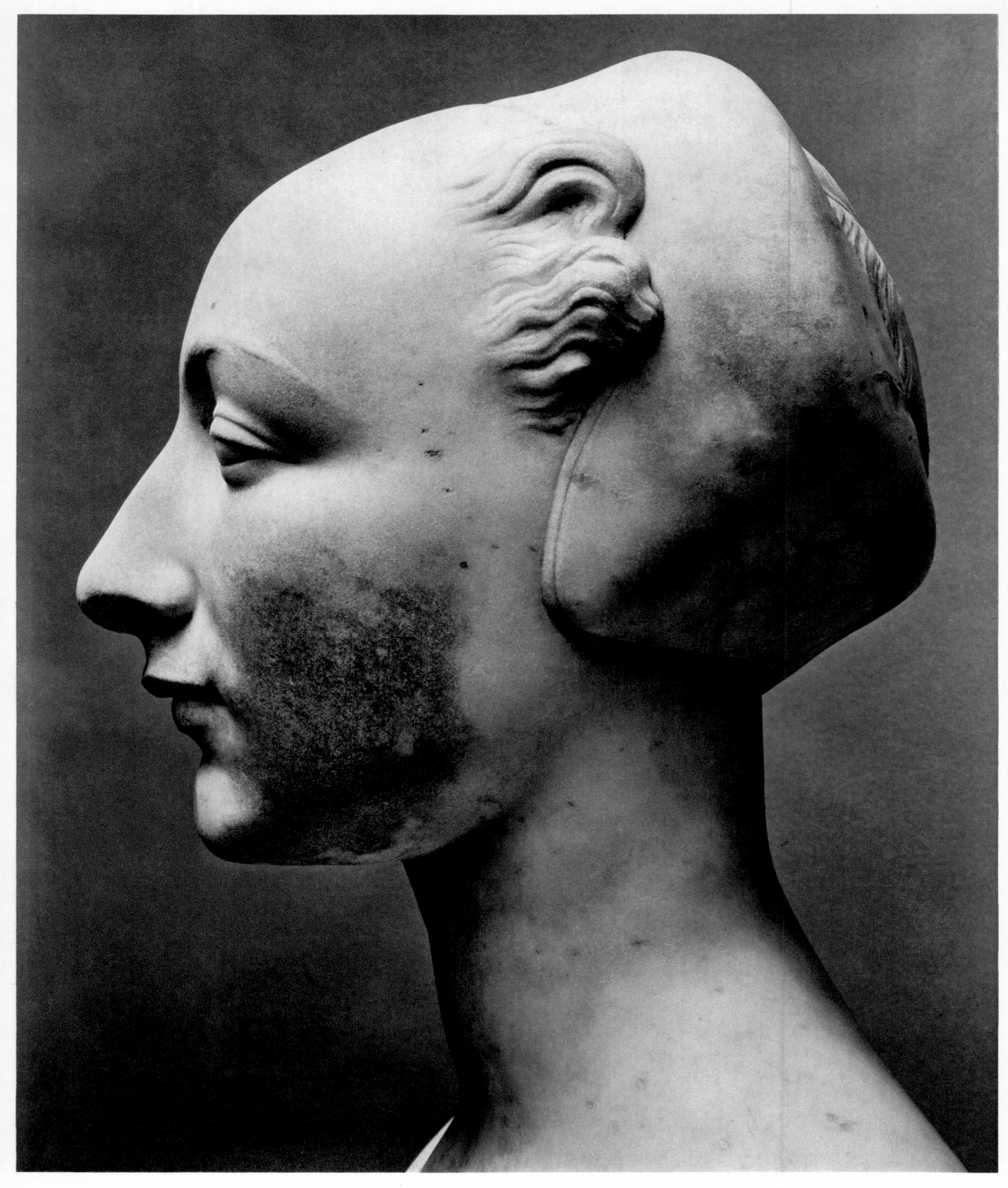

DESIDERIO DA SETTIGNANO · *Bust of a Lady,* Detail. See Page 86

FRANCESCO DA LAURANA · *A Princess of the House of Aragon*, Detail. See Page 87

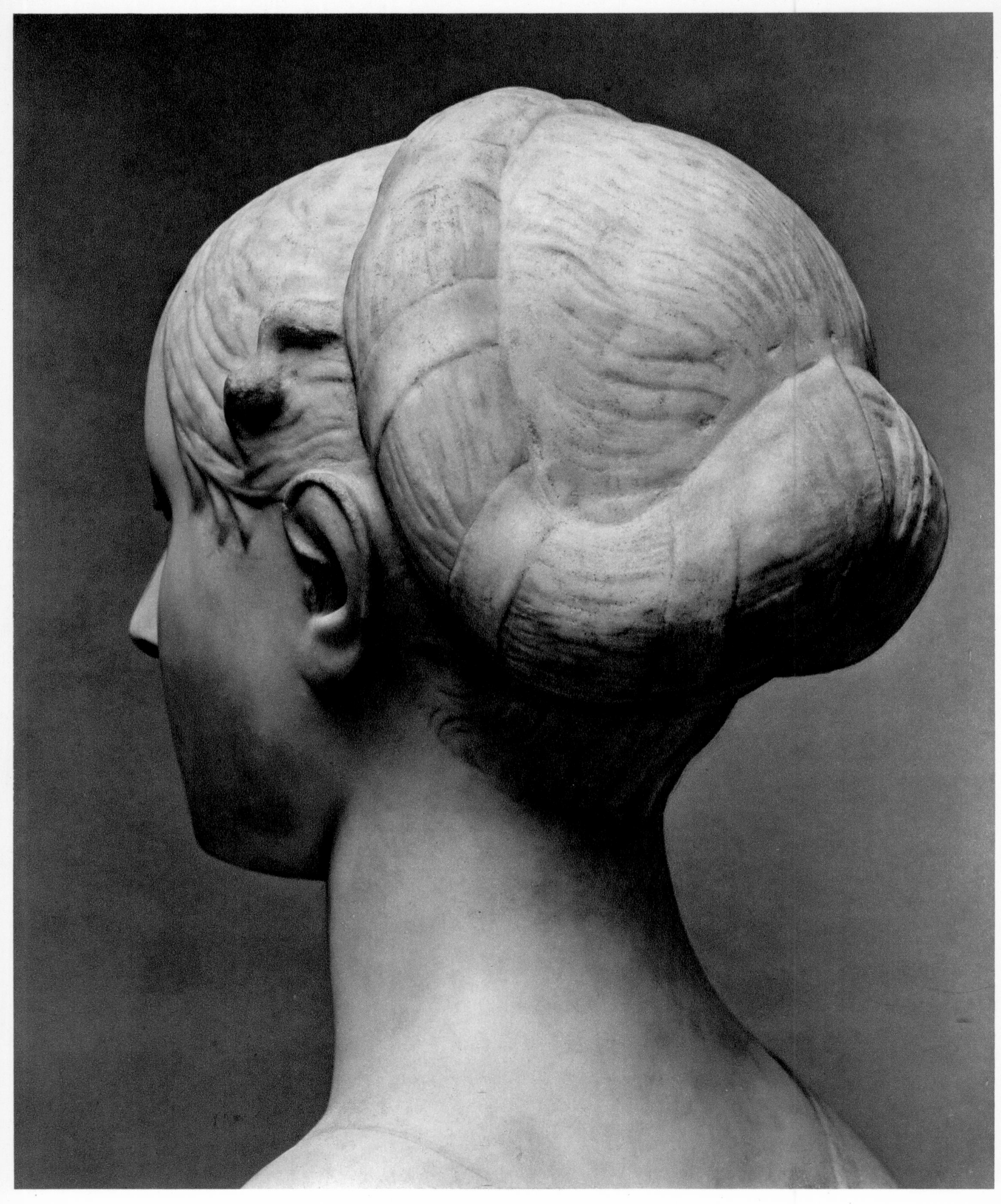

FRANCESCO DA LAURANA · *A Princess of the House of Aragon,* Detail. See Page 87

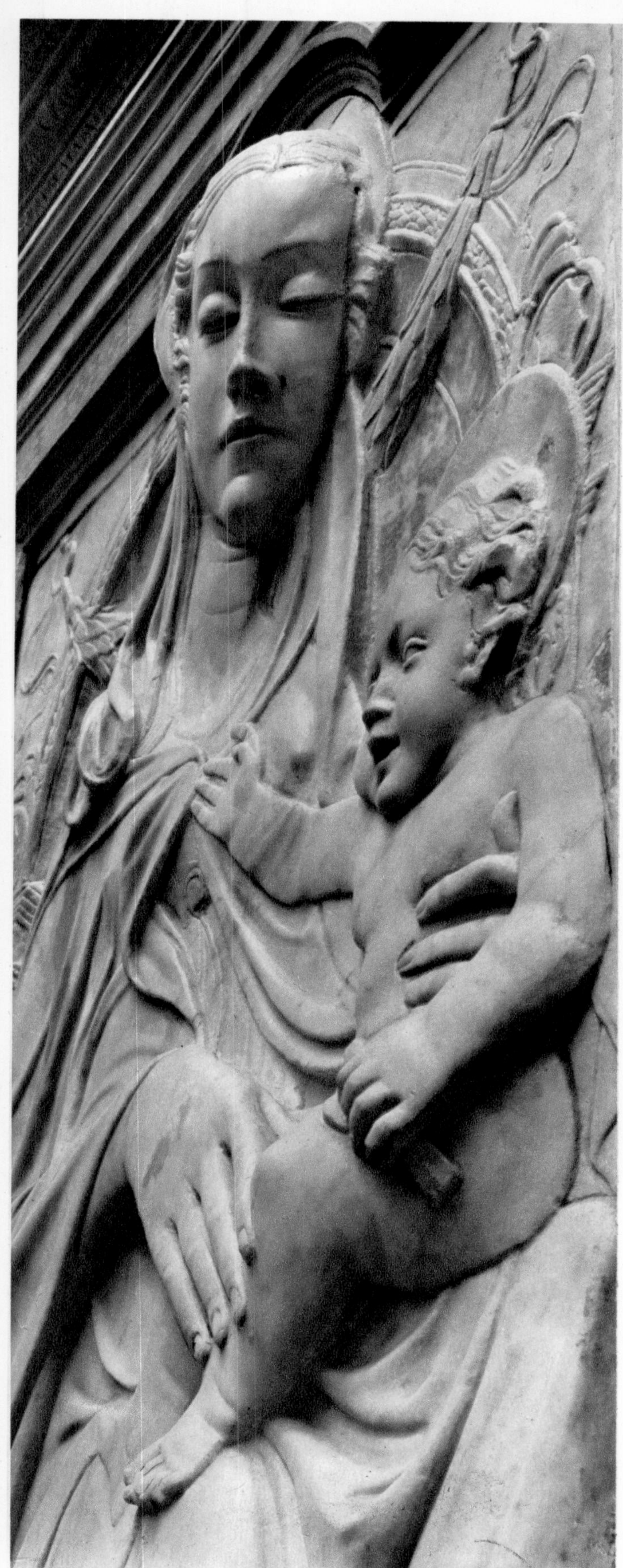

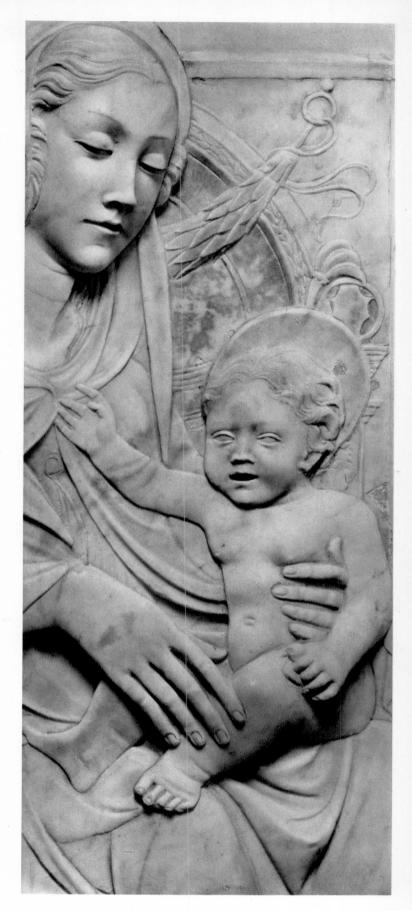

AGOSTINO DI DUCCIO · *Madonna and Child,* Details. See Page 92

Marble H. 28 in.

AGOSTINO DI DUCCIO · *Madonna and Child.* *Mellon Collection.* See Note 25

AGOSTINO DI DUCCIO · *Madonna and Child,* Detail. See Page 92

AGOSTINO DI DUCCIO · *Madonna and Child,* Detail. See Page 92

Marble H. 20 in.

MINO DA FIESOLE · *Virgin Annunciate.* *Kress Collection.* See Note 26

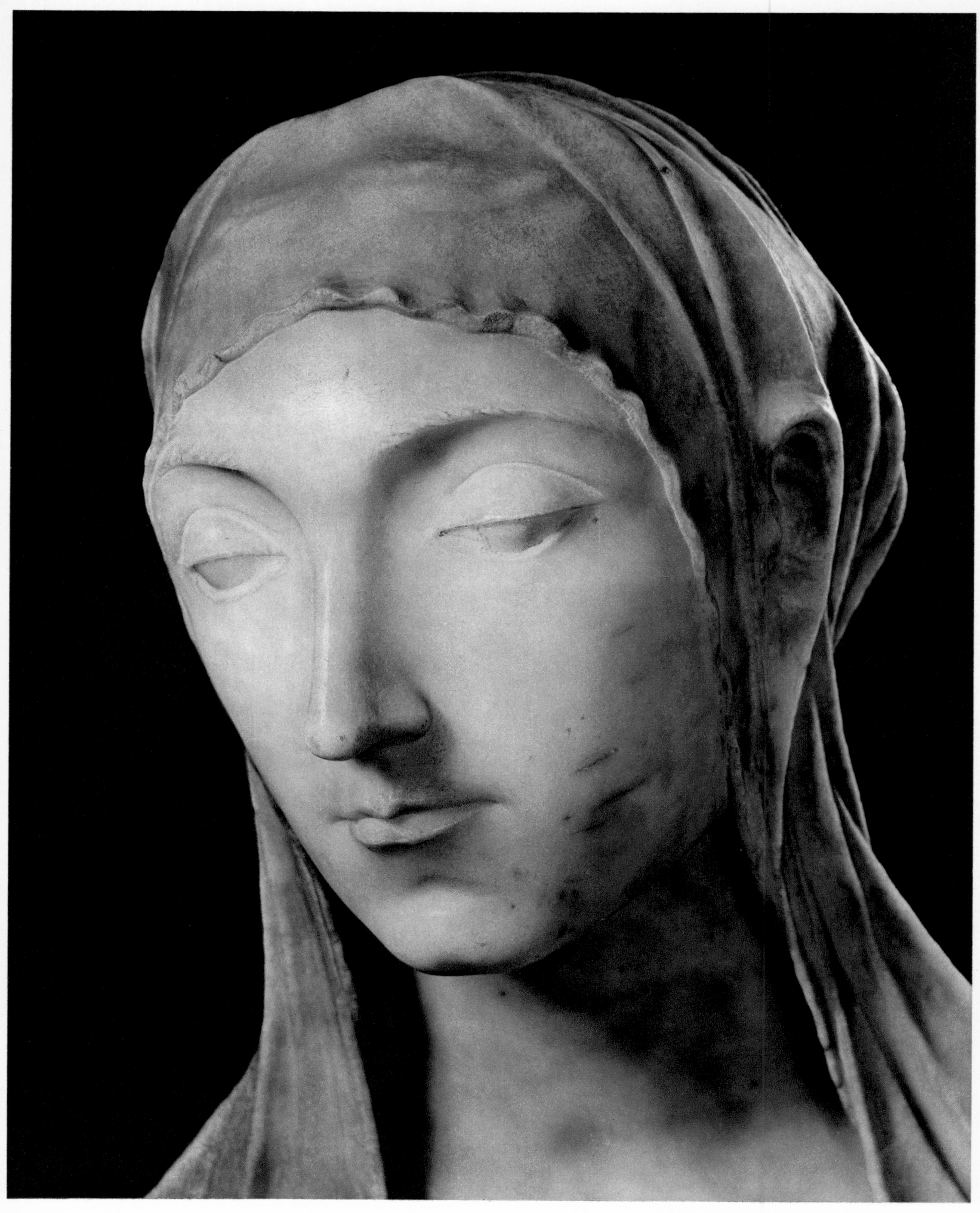

MINO DA FIESOLE · *Virgin Annunciate,* Detail. See Page 95

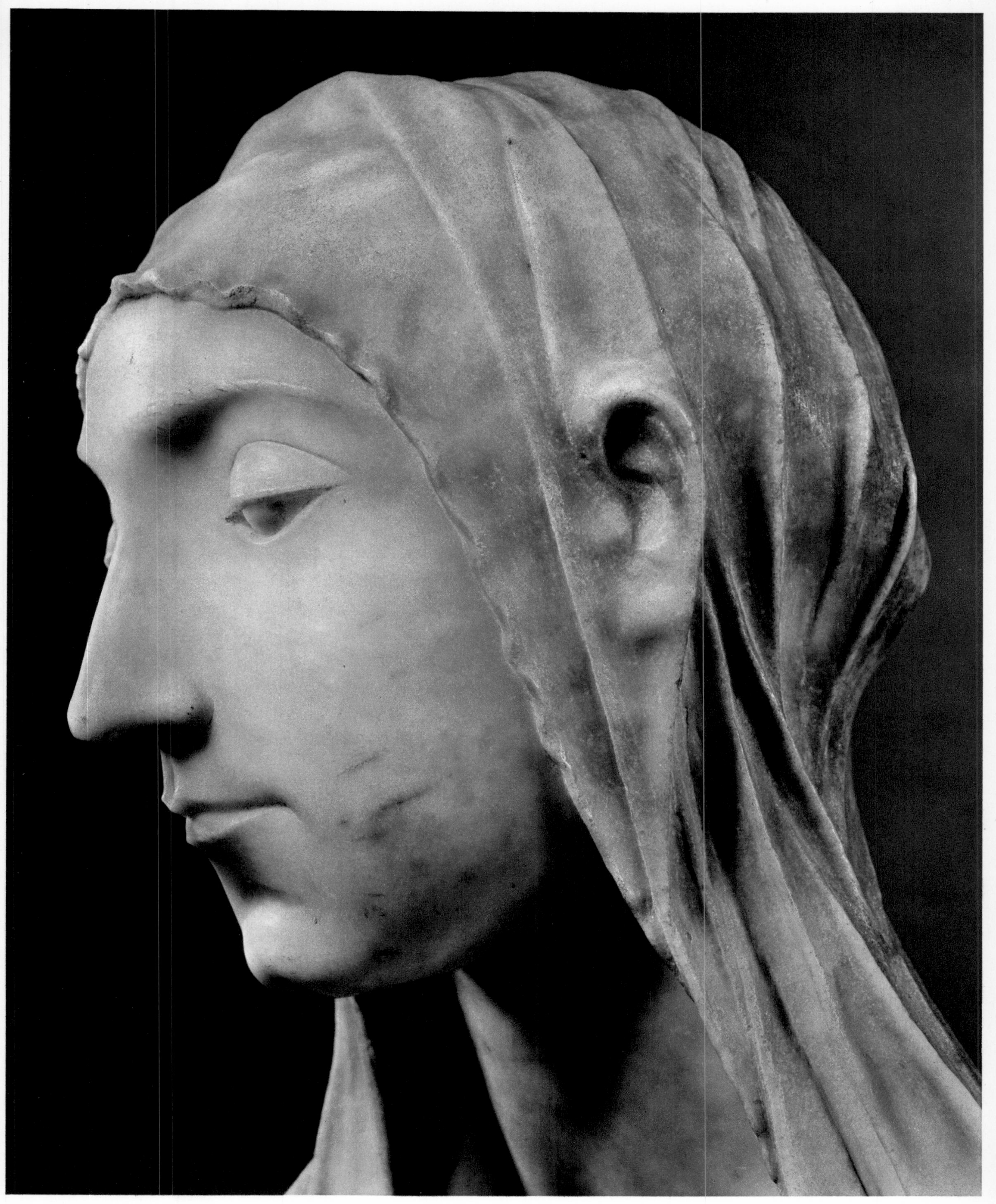

MINO DA FIESOLE · *Virgin Annunciate,* Detail. See Page 95

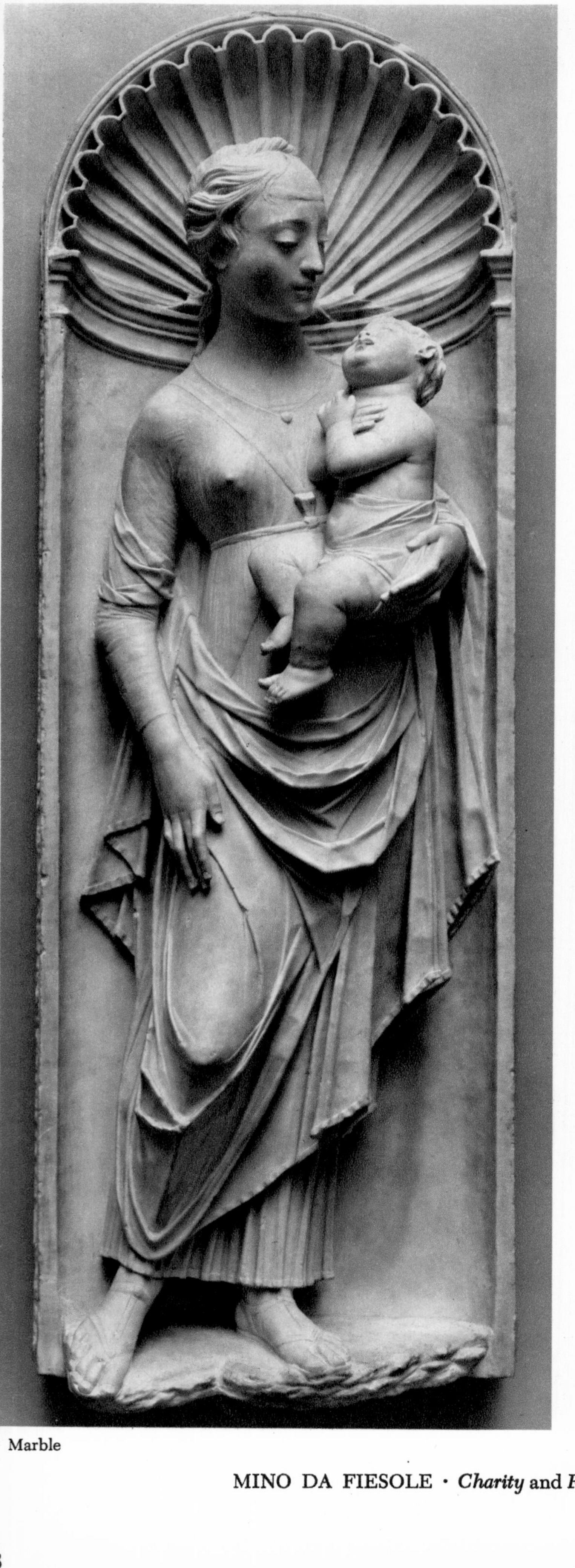

Marble

H. 49¾ in.

MINO DA FIESOLE · *Charity* and *Faith*. *Mellon Collection.* See Notes 27, 28

MINO DA FIESOLE · *Faith,* Detail. See Page 98

MINO DA FIESOLE · *Charity*, Detail. See Page 98

MINO DA FIESOLE · *Faith,* Detail. See Page 98

Marble H. 16¾ in.

DESIDERIO DA SETTIGNANO · *Saint Jerome in the Desert.* *Widener Collection.* See Note 29

DESIDERIO DA SETTIGNANO · *Saint Jerome in the Desert*, Detail. See Page 102

DESIDERIO DA SETTIGNANO · *Saint Jerome in the Desert,* Detail. See Page 102

DESIDERIO DA SETTIGNANO · *Saint Jerome in the Desert*, Detail. See Page 102

Bronze

H. 21⅝ in.

FRANCESCO DI GIORGIO · *Saint Jerome.* *Kress Collection, Loan.* See Note 30

Bronze

Enlarged

FRANCESCO DI GIORGIO · *Judgment of Paris.* *Kress Collection, Loan.* See Note 31

Bronze Diam. 8 in.

FRANCESCO DI GIORGIO · *Saint Sebastian.* *Kress Collection, Loan.* See Note 32

MATTEO CIVITALE · *Saint Sebastian,* Detail. See Page 110

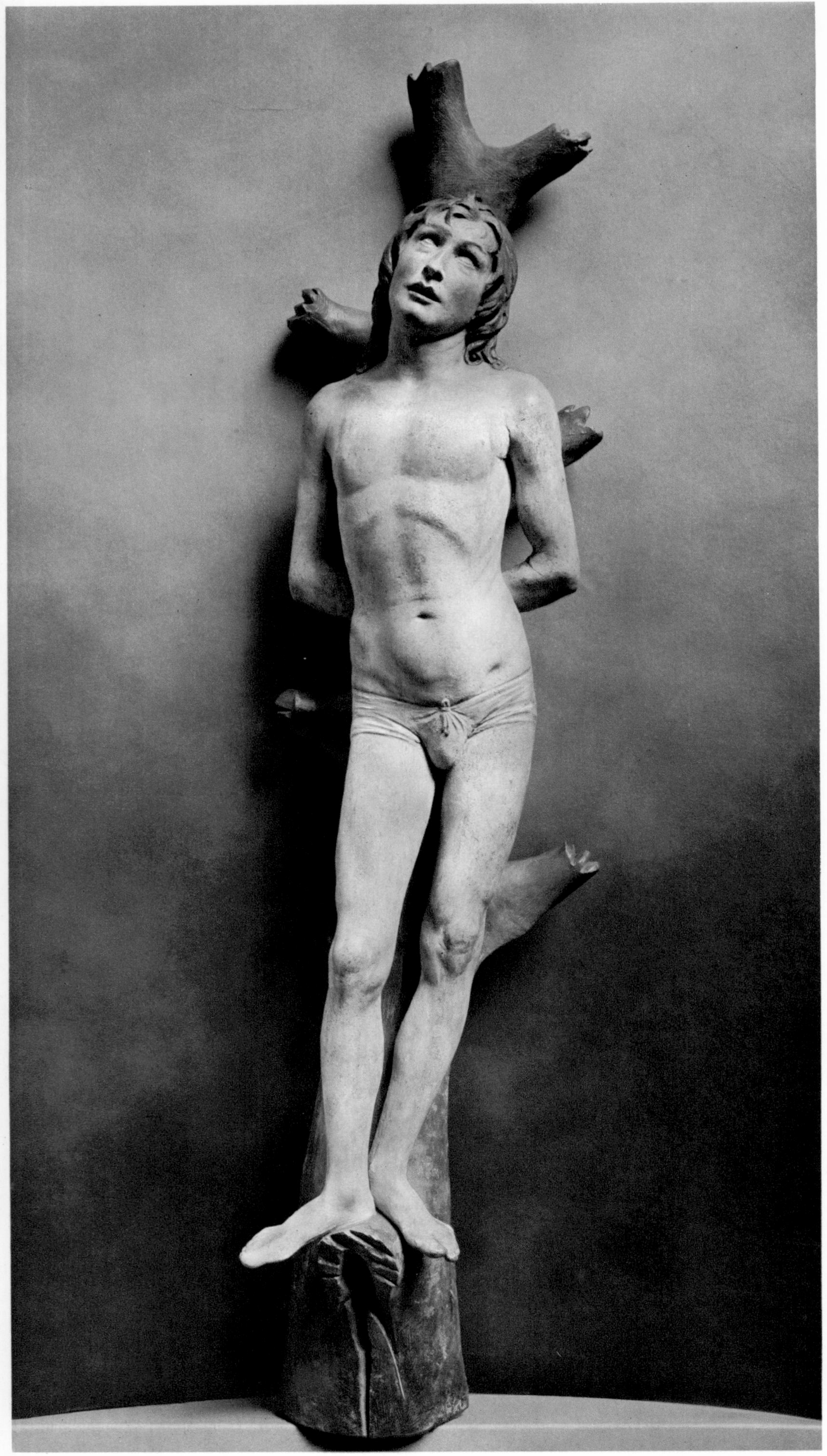

Painted terra cotta H. 25⅝ in.

MATTEO CIVITALE · *Saint Sebastian.* *Kress Collection.* See Note 33

Painted terra cotta H. 29½ in.

ANDREA DEL VERROCCHIO · *Putto Poised on a Globe.* *Mellon Collection.* See Note 34

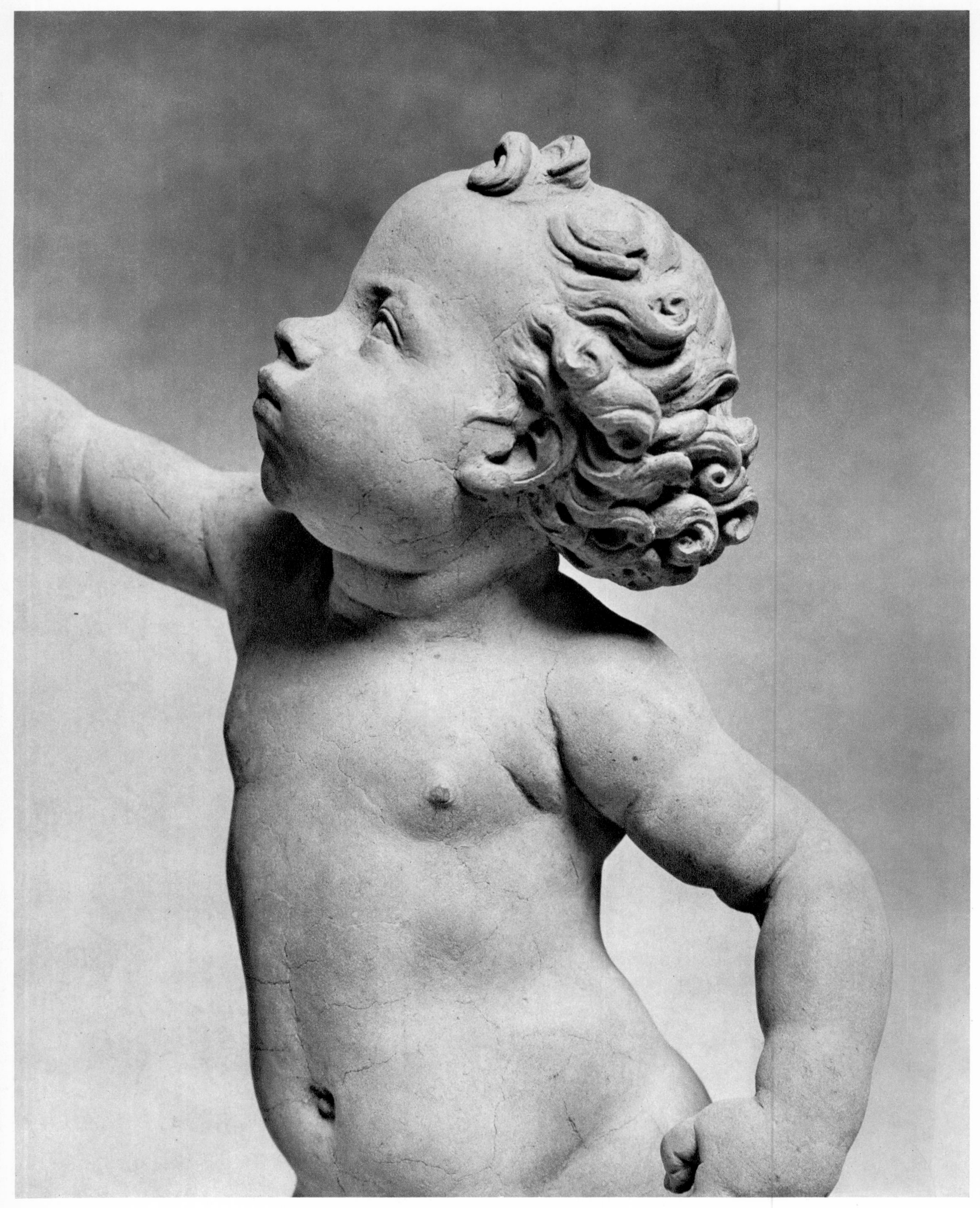

ANDREA DEL VERROCCHIO · *Putto Poised on a Globe,* Detail. See Page 111

ANDREA DEL VERROCCHIO · *Giuliano de' Medici,* Detail. See Page 114

Painted terra cotta H. 24 in.

ANDREA DEL VERROCCHIO · *Giuliano de' Medici.* *Mellon Collection.* See Note 35

ANDREA DEL VERROCCHIO · *Giuliano de' Medici,* Detail. See Page 114

ANDREA DEL VERROCCHIO · *Giuliano de' Medici,* Detail. See Page 114

ANDREA DEL VERROCCHIO · *Lorenzo de' Medici,* Detail. See Page 118

Painted terra cotta H. 25⅞ in.

ANDREA DEL VERROCCHIO · *Lorenzo de' Medici.* *Kress Collection.* See Note 36

ANDREA DEL VERROCCHIO · *Lorenzo de' Medici,* Detail. See Page 118

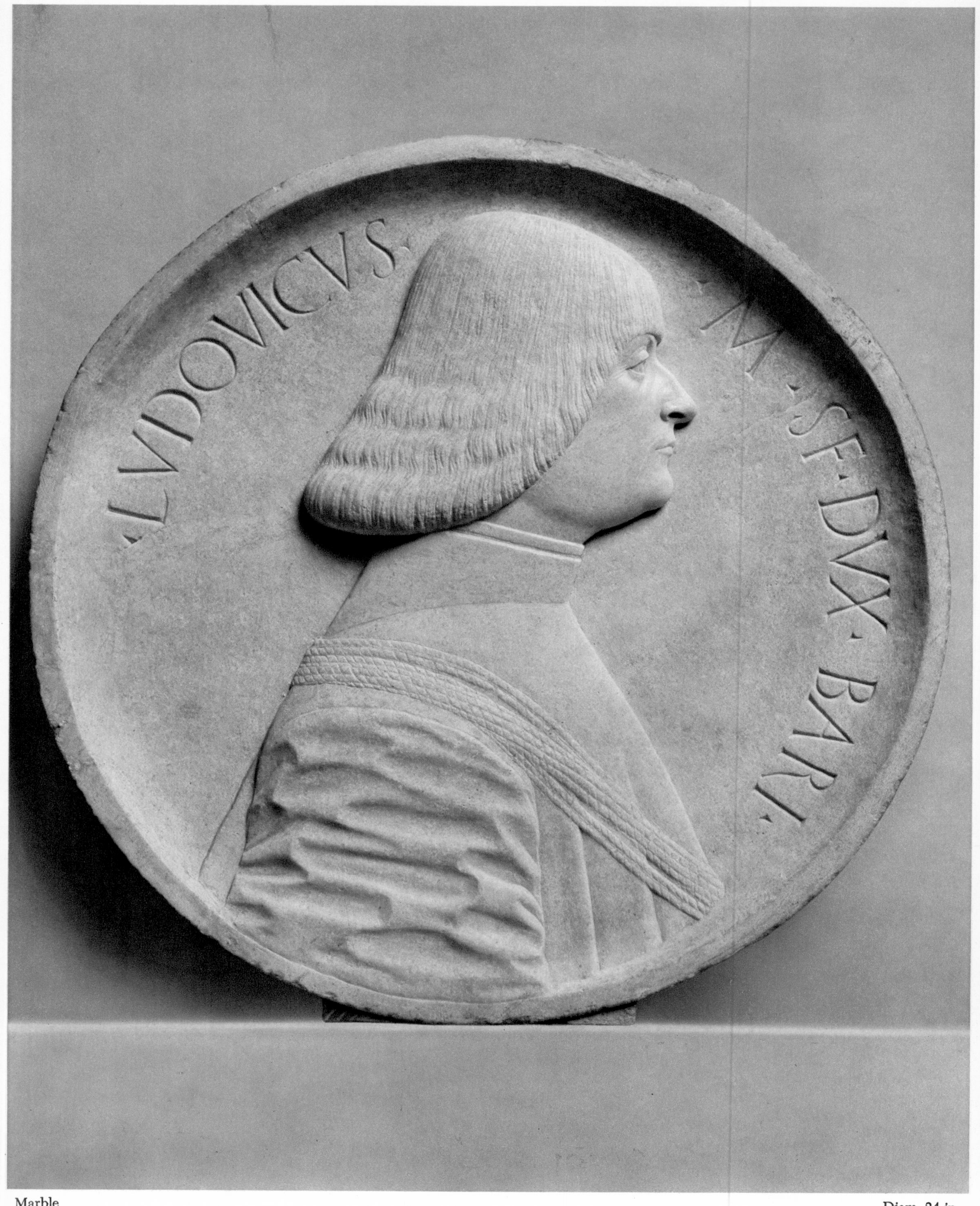

Marble

Diam. 24 in.

GIOVANNI ANTONIO AMADEO · *Lodovico Sforza, Called Il Moro.* *Mellon Collection.* See Note 37

Bronze | Enlarged

ALBERTI (?) · *Portrait of Leone Battista Alberti.* *Kress Collection.* See Note 38

Marble H. 19¾ in.

CRISTOFORO SOLARI · *Madonna and Child.* *Kress Collection.* See Note 39

CRISTOFORO SOLARI · *Madonna and Child,* Detail. See Page 122

Marble H. 33⅞ in.

PIETRO LOMBARDO · *A Singing Angel.* *Kress Collection.* See Note 40

PIETRO LOMBARDO · *A Singing Angel,* Detail. See Page 124

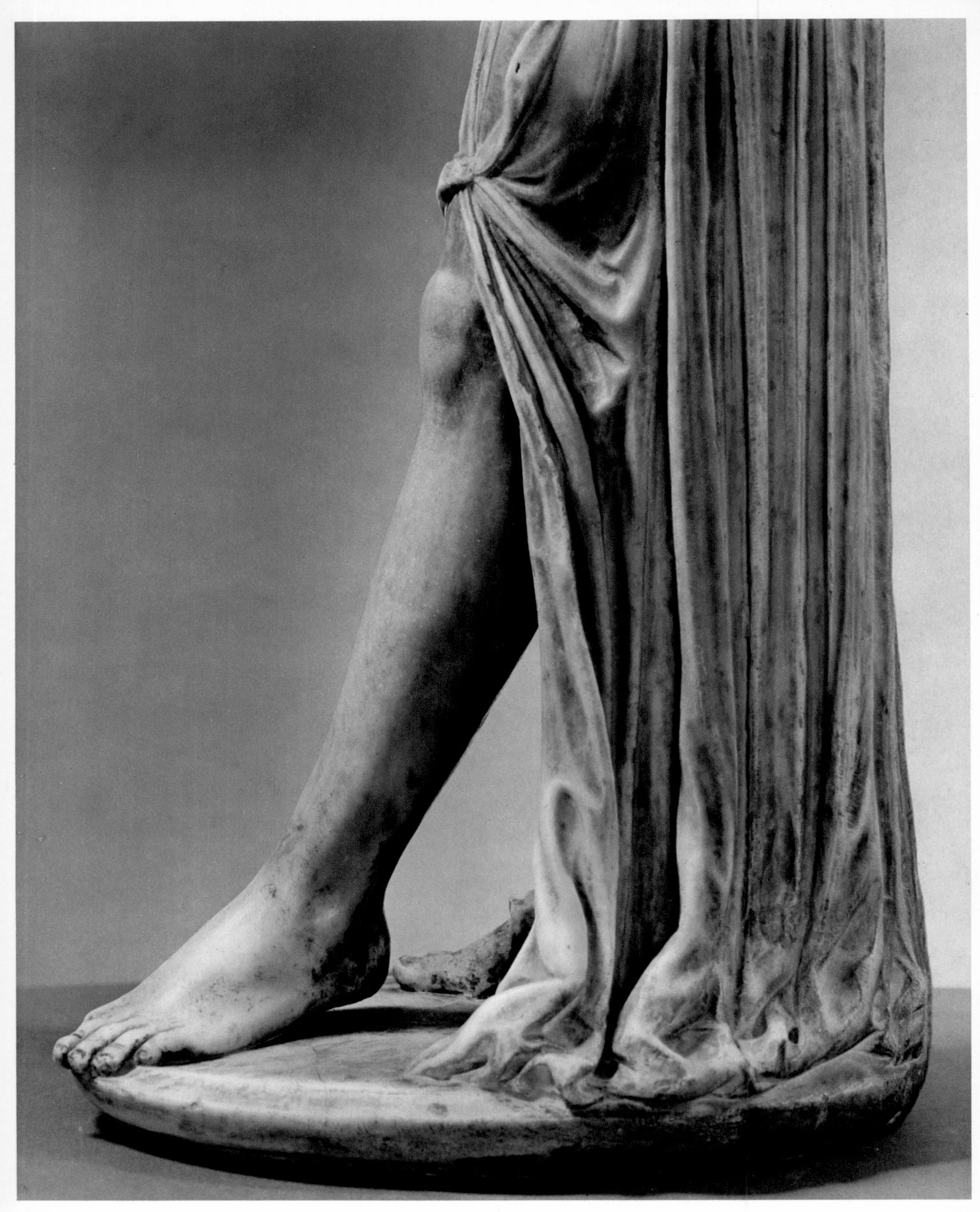

PIETRO LOMBARDO · *A Singing Angel,* Detail. See Page 124

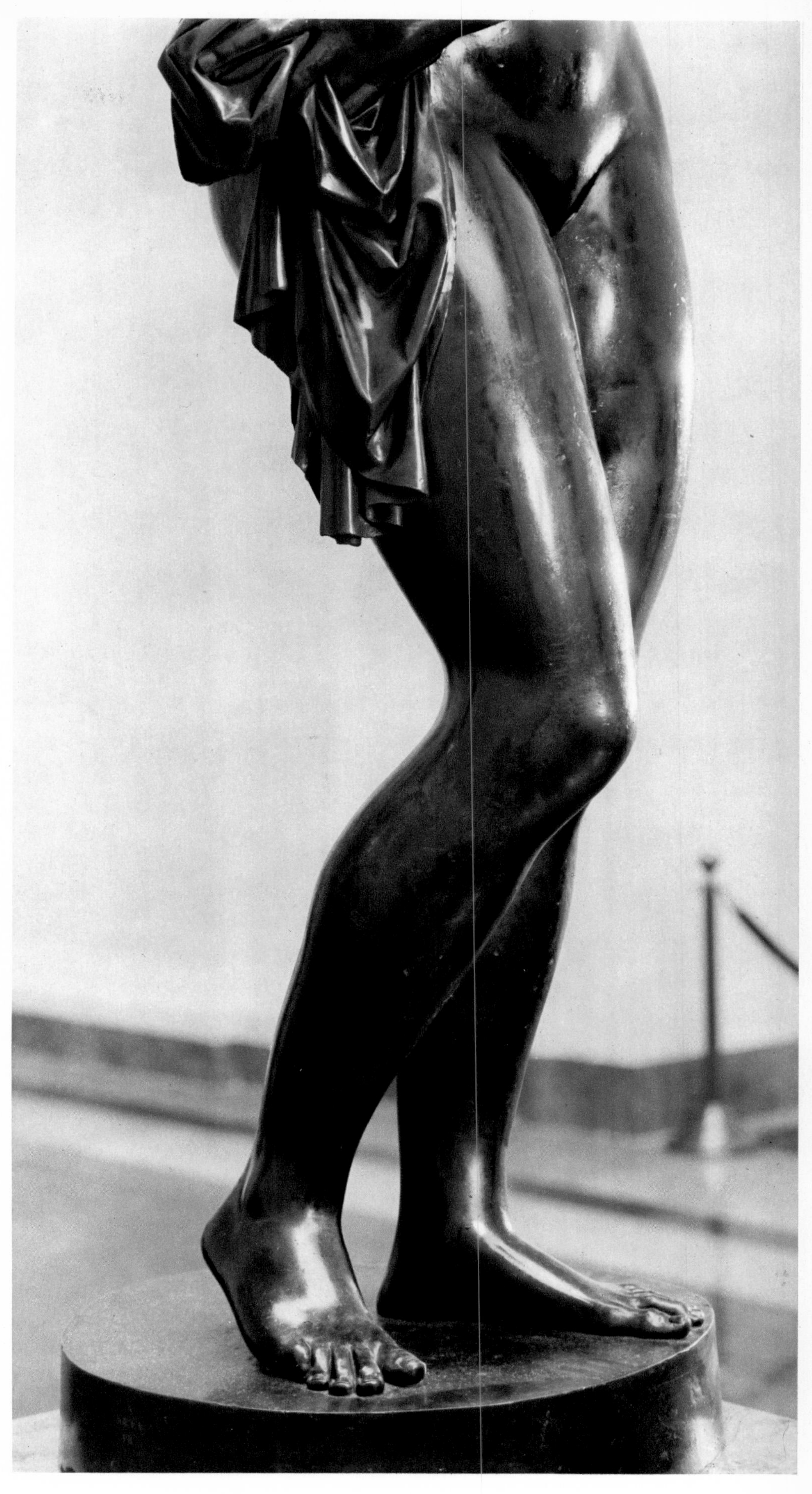

JACOPO SANSOVINO · *Venus Anadyomene,* Detail. See Page 129

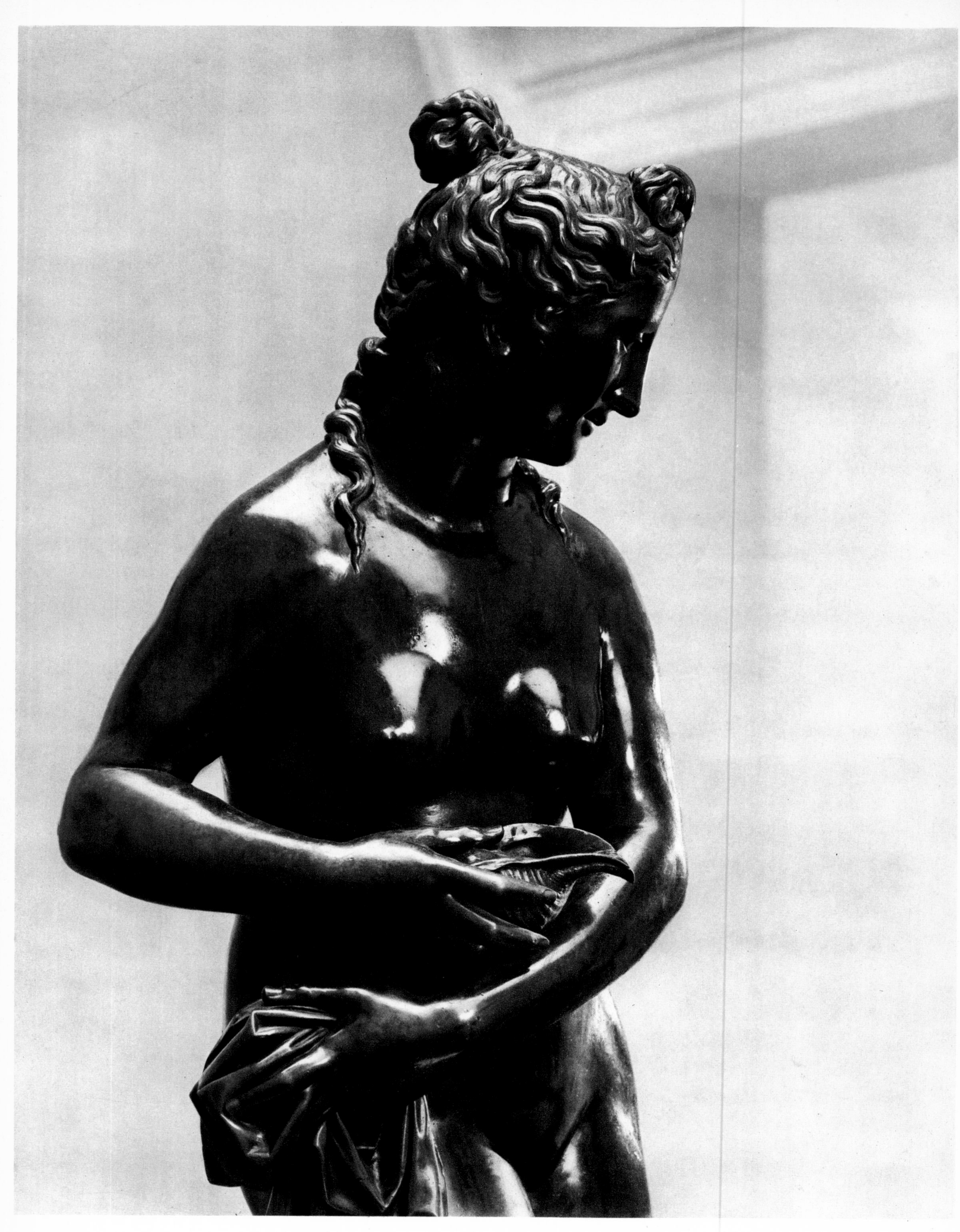

JACOPO SANSOVINO · *Venus Anadyomene,* Detail. See Page 129

Bronze H. 65⅞ in.

JACOPO SANSOVINO · *Venus Anadyomene. Mellon Collection.* See Note 41

Bronze

H. 19$\frac{13}{16}$ in.

ANDREA RICCIO · *The Entombment.* *Kress Collection, Loan.* See Note 42

ANDREA RICCIO · *The Entombment,* Detail. See Page 130

ANDREA RICCIO · *The Entombment,* Detail. See Page 130

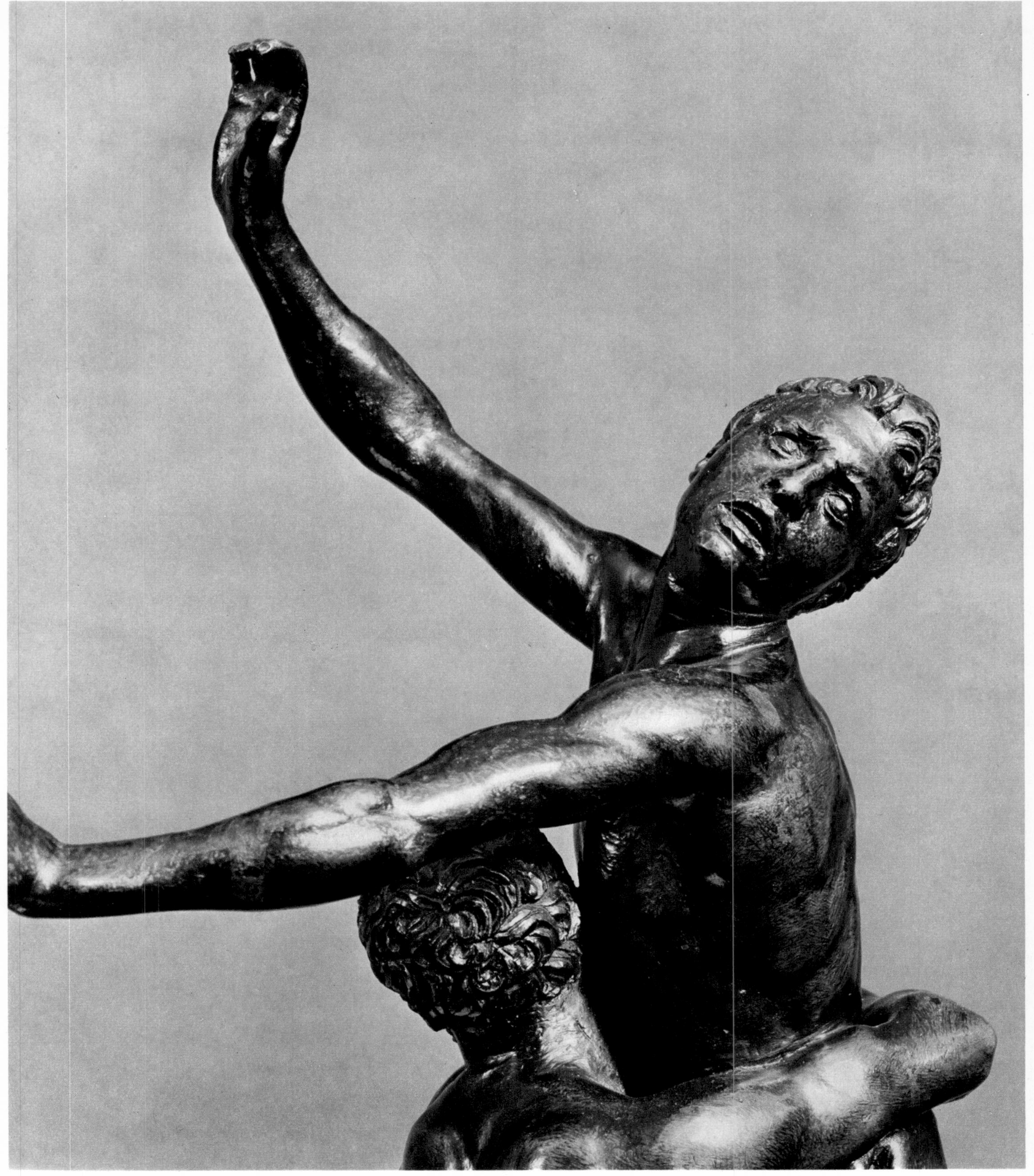

FRANCESCO DA SANT'AGATA · *Hercules and Antaeus*, Detail. See Pages 134, 135

Bronze

H. 15$\frac{1}{16}$ in.

FRANCESCO DA SANT'AGATA · *Hercules and Antaeus.* *Widener Collection.* See Note 43

Bronze

H. 15⅟₁₆ in.

FRANCESCO DA SANT'AGATA · *Hercules and Antaeus.* *Widener Collection.* See Note 43

Bronze H. 17½ in.

VINCENZO DANTI · *Descent from the Cross.* *Widener Collection.* See Note 44

VINCENZO DANTI · *Descent from the Cross,* Detail. See Page 136

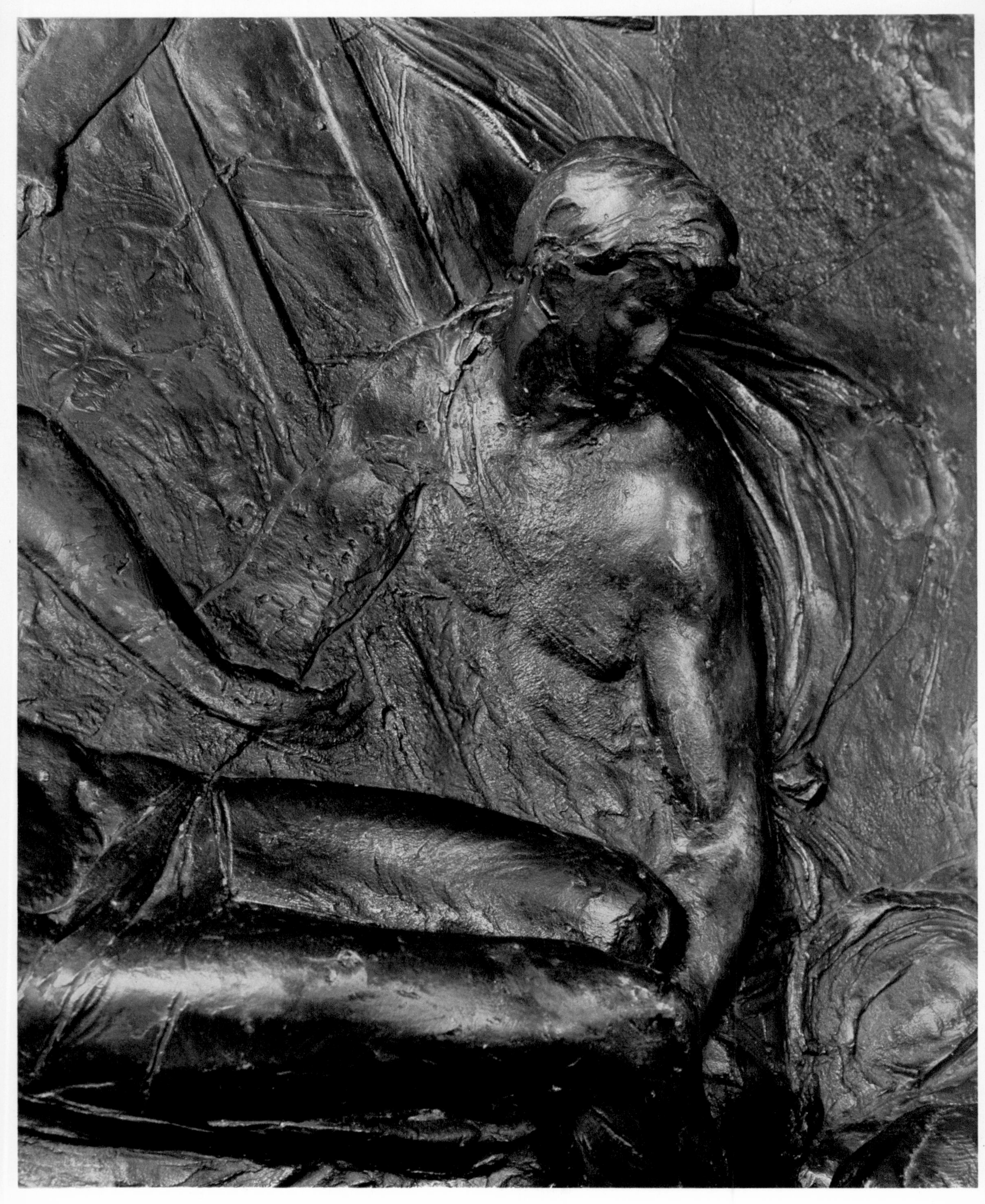

VINCENZO DANTI · *Descent from the Cross,* Detail. See Page 136

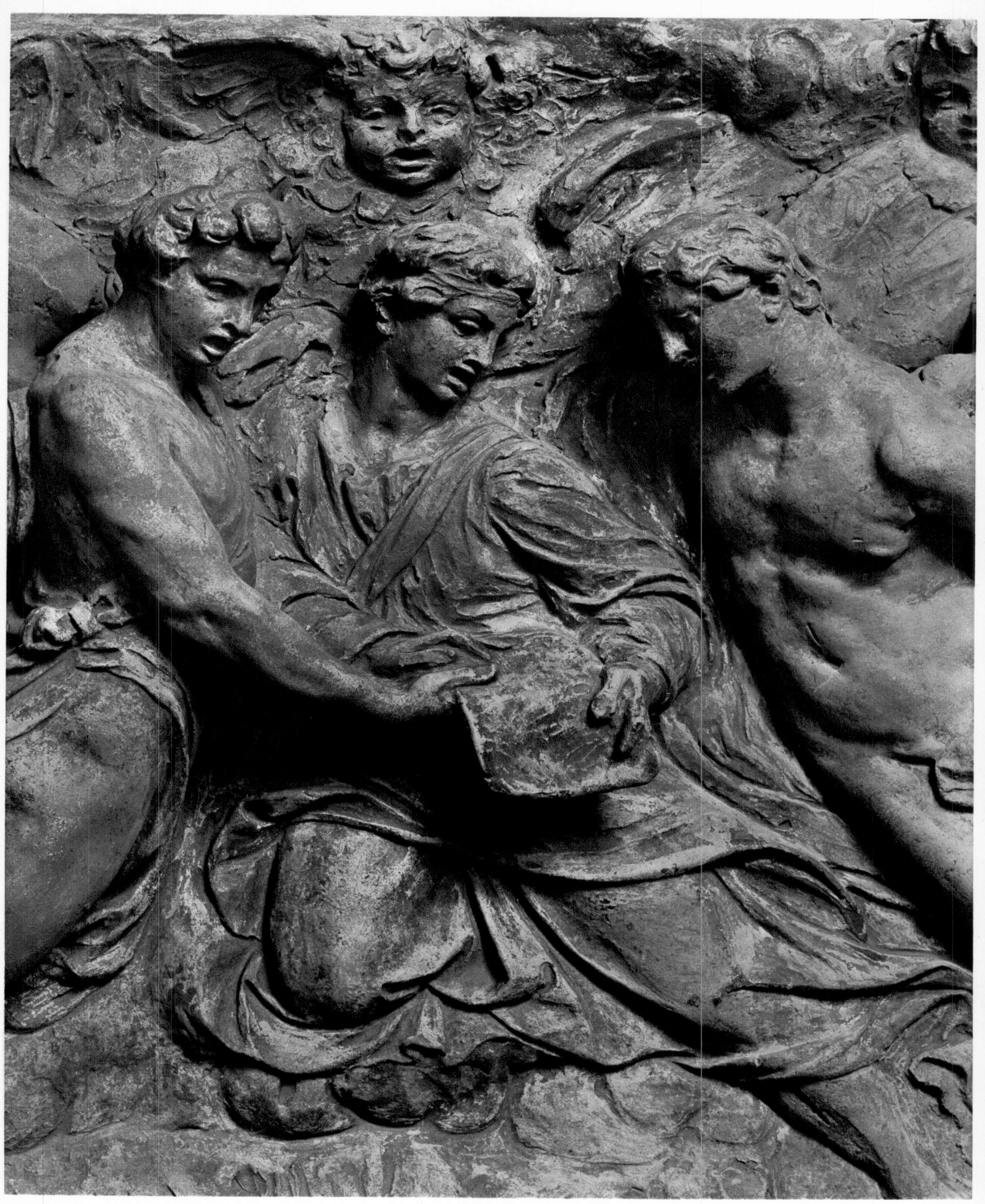

ANNIBALE FONTANA · *Adoration of the Shepherds,* Detail. See Page 140

Terra cotta H. 43 in.

ANNIBALE FONTANA · *Adoration of the Shepherds.* *Kress Collection.* See Note 45

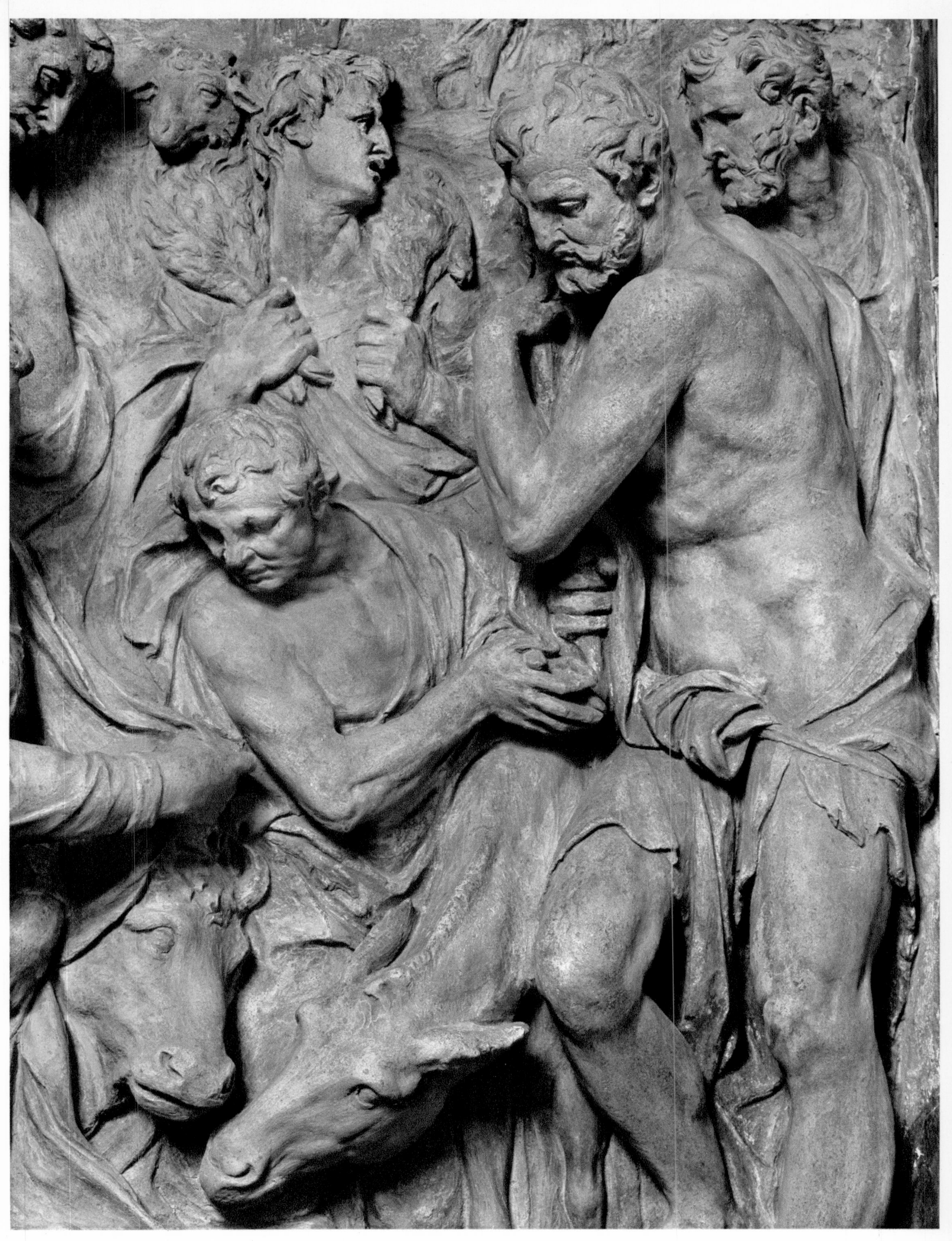

ANNIBALE FONTANA · *Adoration of the Shepherds,* Detail. See Page 140

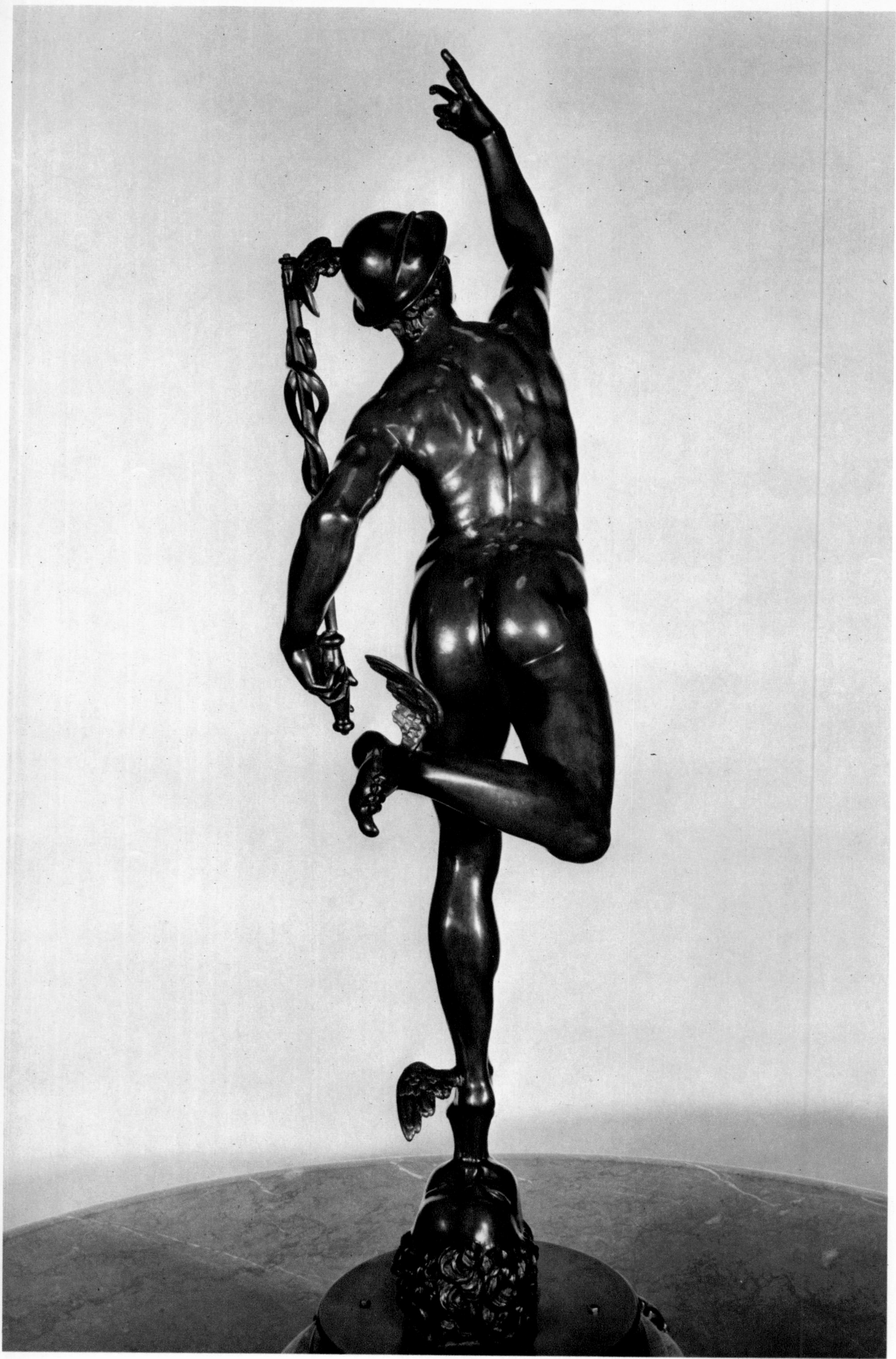

Bronze

H. 69⅝ in.

GIOVANNI BOLOGNA · *Mercury.* *Mellon Collection.* See Note 46

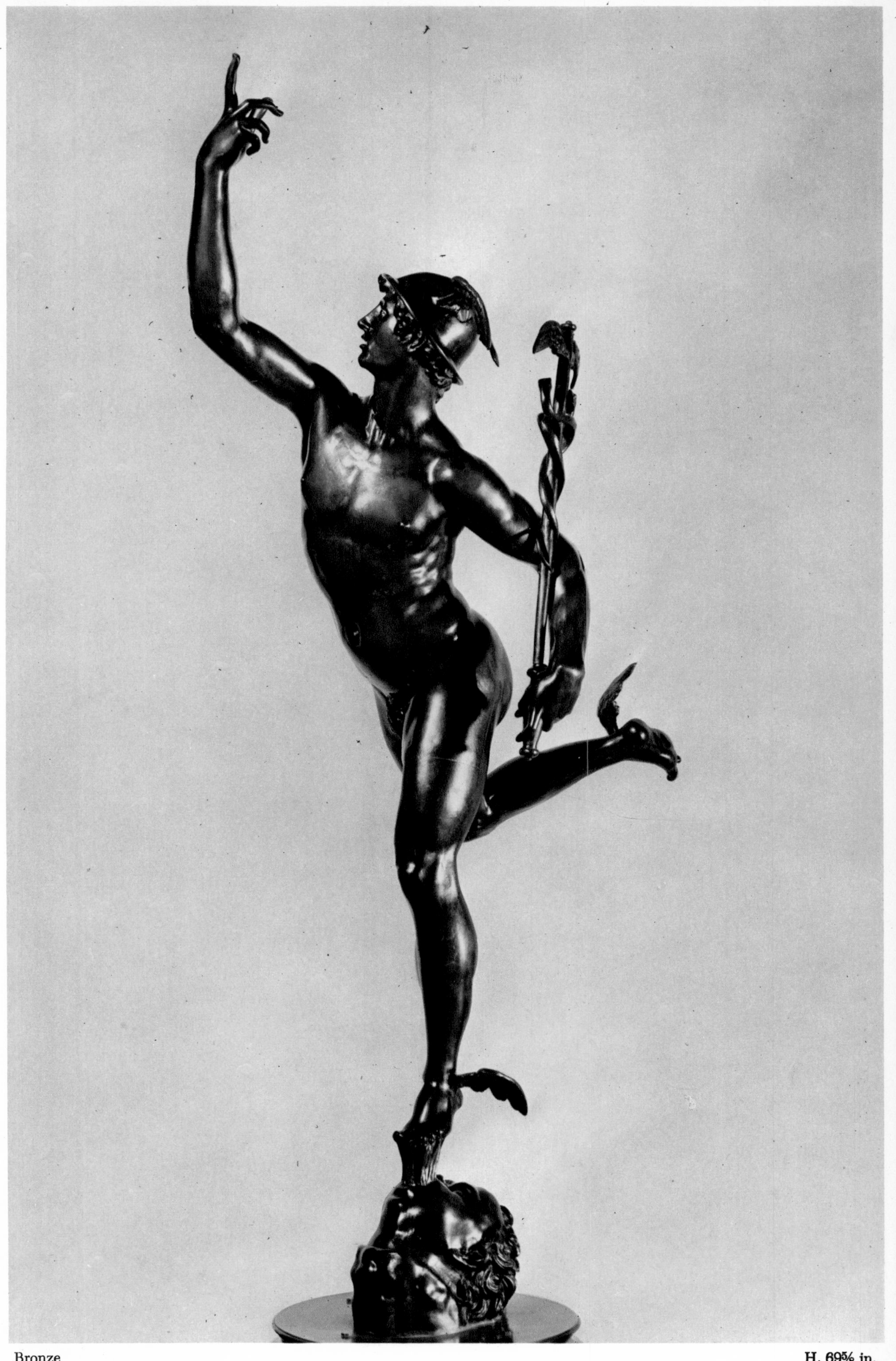

Bronze H. 69⅝ in.

GIOVANNI BOLOGNA · *Mercury.* *Mellon Collection.* See Note 46

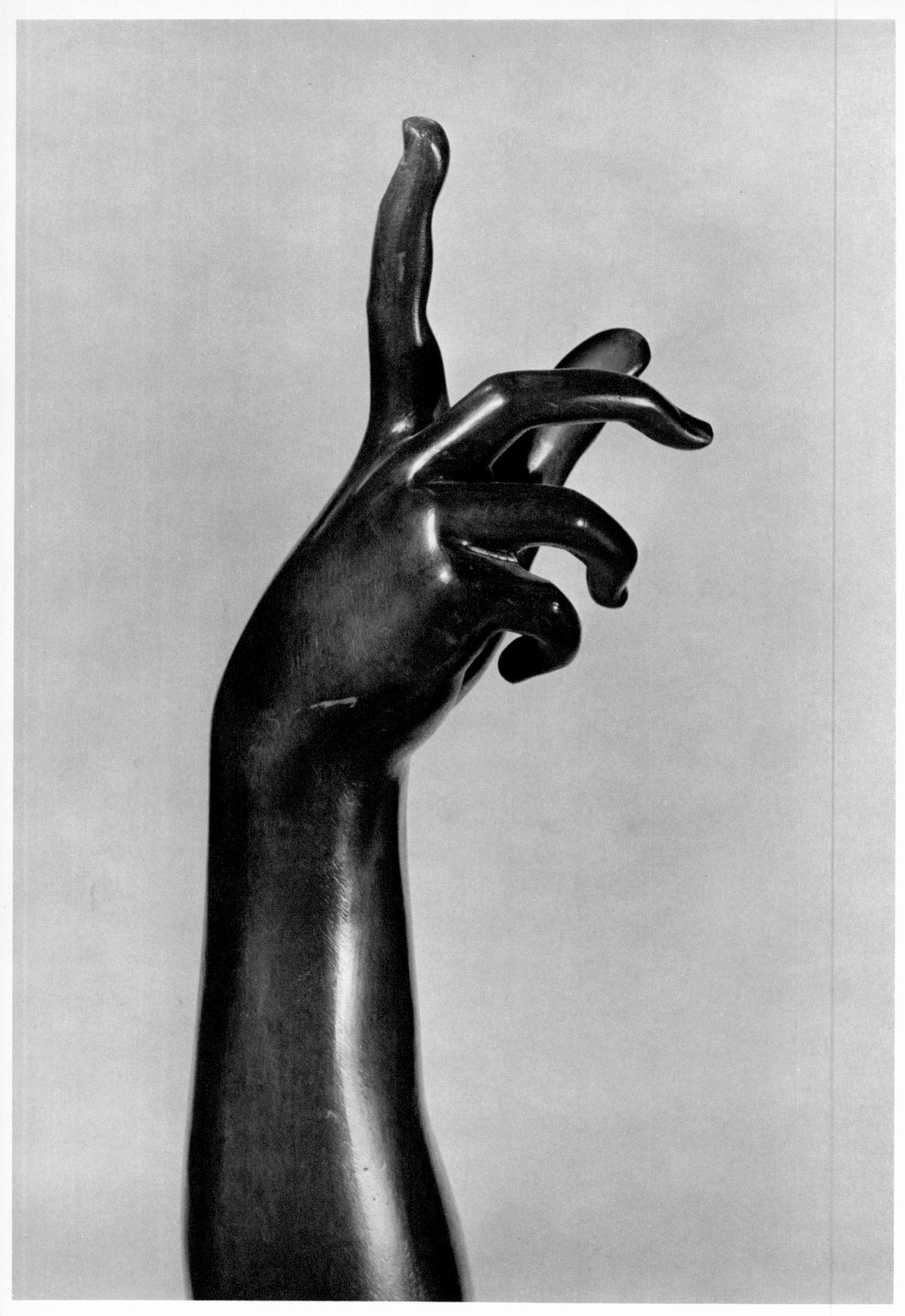

GIOVANNI BOLOGNA · *Mercury*, Detail. See Pages 142, 143

GIOVANNI BOLOGNA · *Mercury,* Detail. See Pages 142, 143

Bronze H. 9 9/16 in.

BENVENUTO CELLINI · *Virtue Overcoming Vice.* *Widener Collection.* See Note 47

Bronze H. 30 7/16 in.

ADRIAEN DE VRIES · *Virtue and Vice.* *Widener Collection.* See Note 48

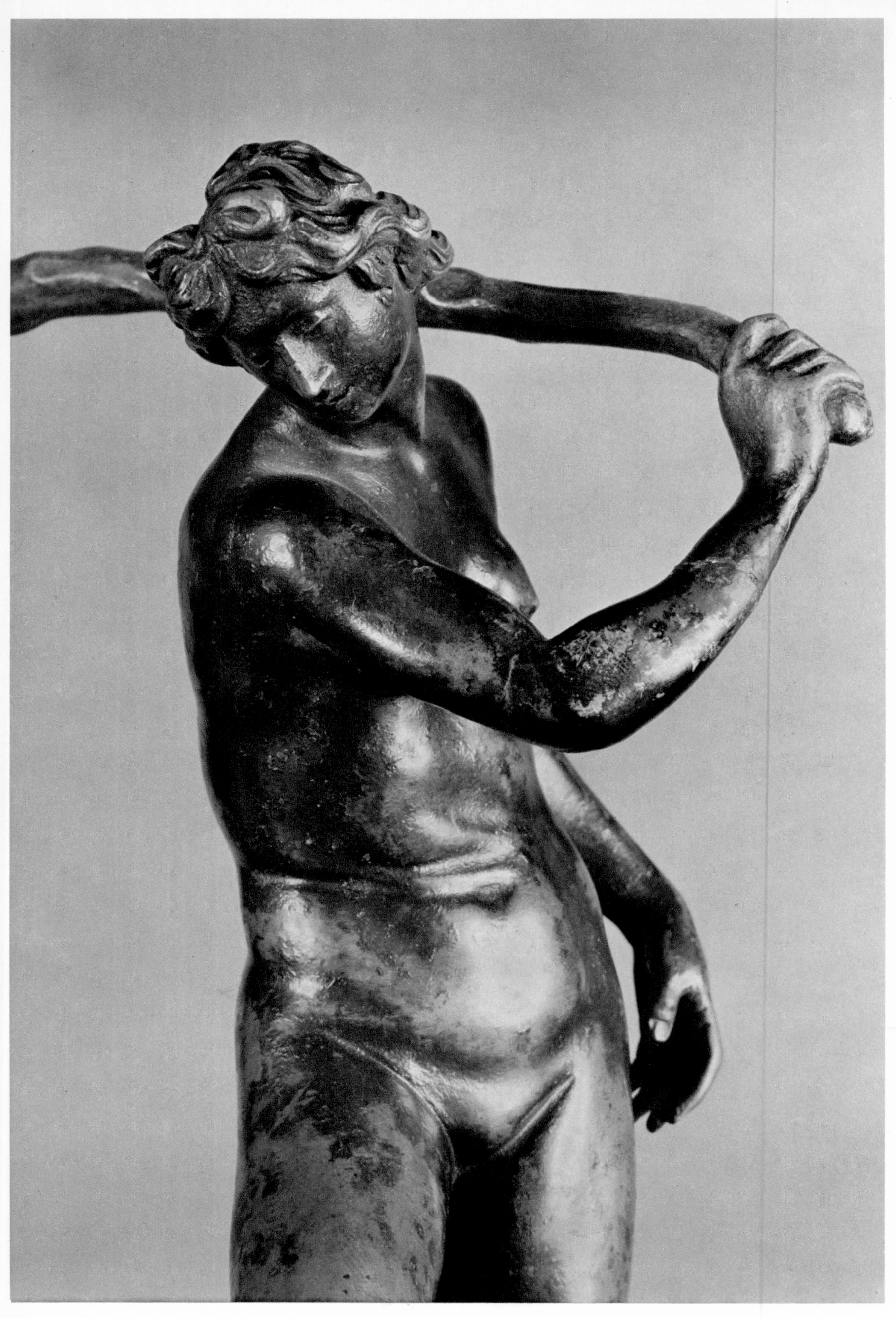

BENVENUTO CELLINI · *Virtue Overcoming Vice,* Detail. See Page 146

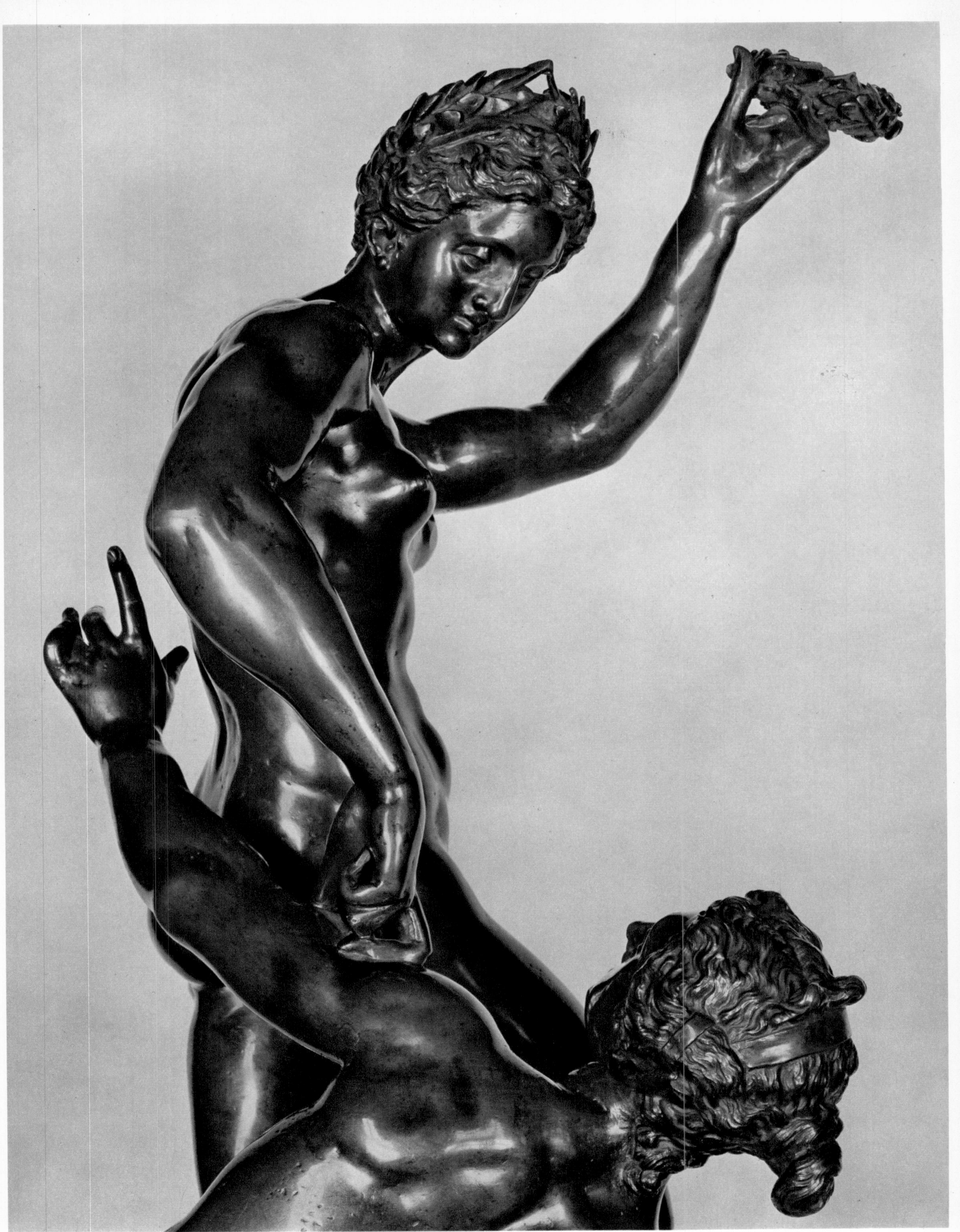

ADRIAEN DE VRIES · *Virtue and Vice,* Detail. See Page 147

ADRIAEN DE VRIES · *Virtue and Vice,* Detail. See Page 147

ADRIAEN DE VRIES · *Virtue and Vice*, Detail. See Page 147

Bronze H. 33⅛ in.

LORENZO BERNINI · *Louis XIV*. *Kress Collection*. See Note 49

LORENZO BERNINI · *Louis XIV*, Detail. See Page 152

Marble H. (with plinth) 71¾ in.

JEAN LOUIS LEMOYNE · *Diana.* *Widener Collection.* See Note 50

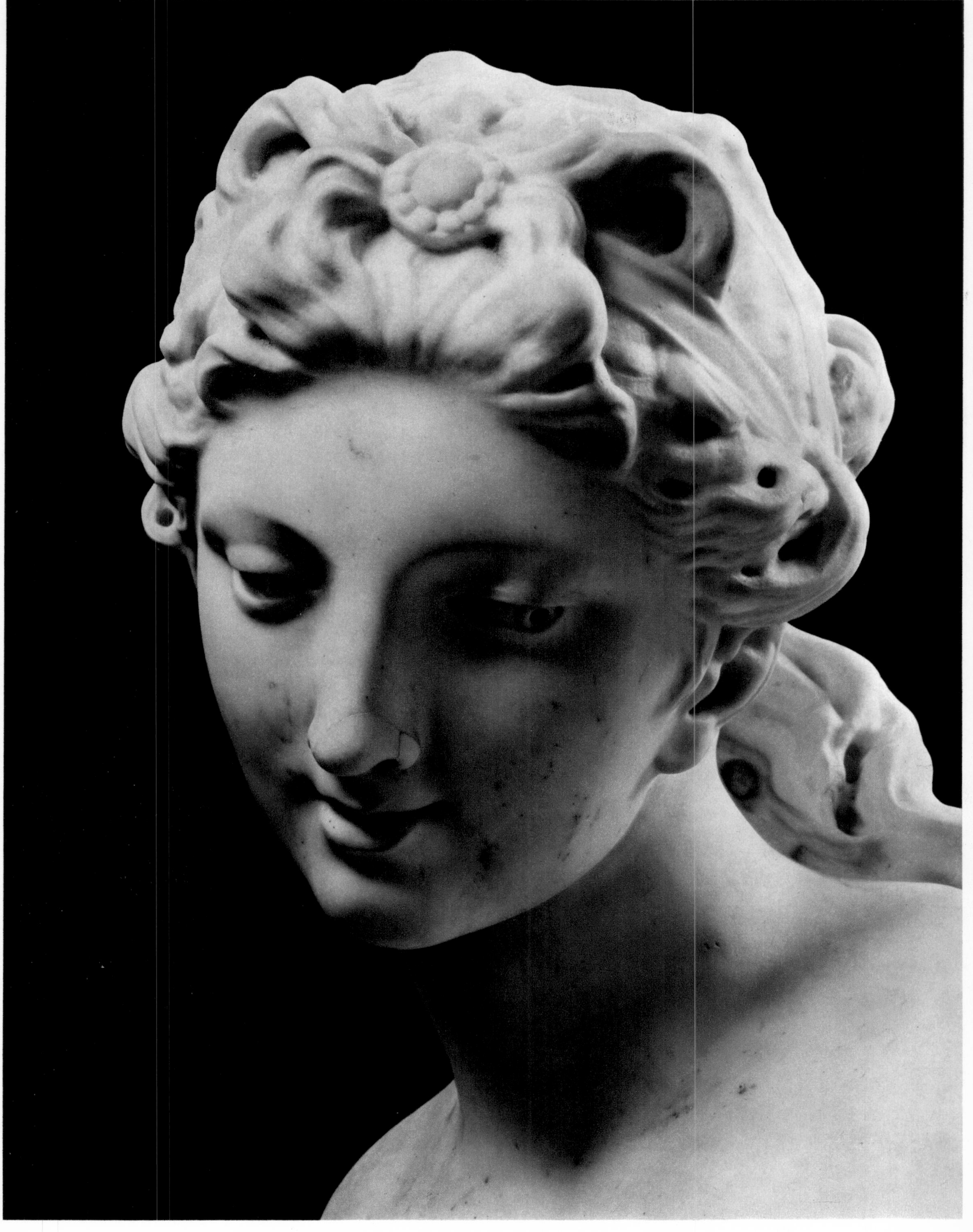

JEAN LOUIS LEMOYNE · *Diana,* Detail. See Page 154

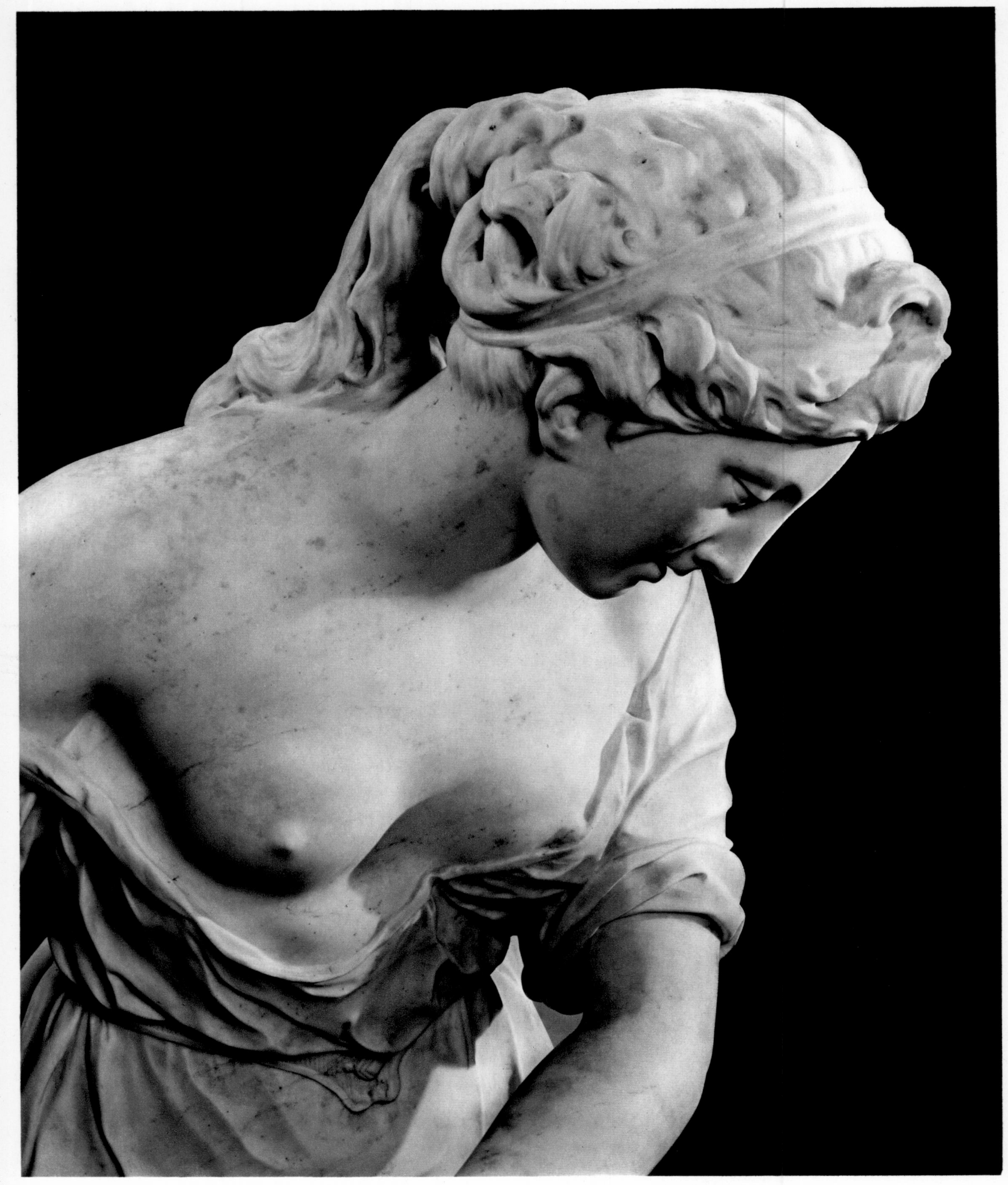

JEAN LOUIS LEMOYNE · *Diana,* Detail. See Page 154

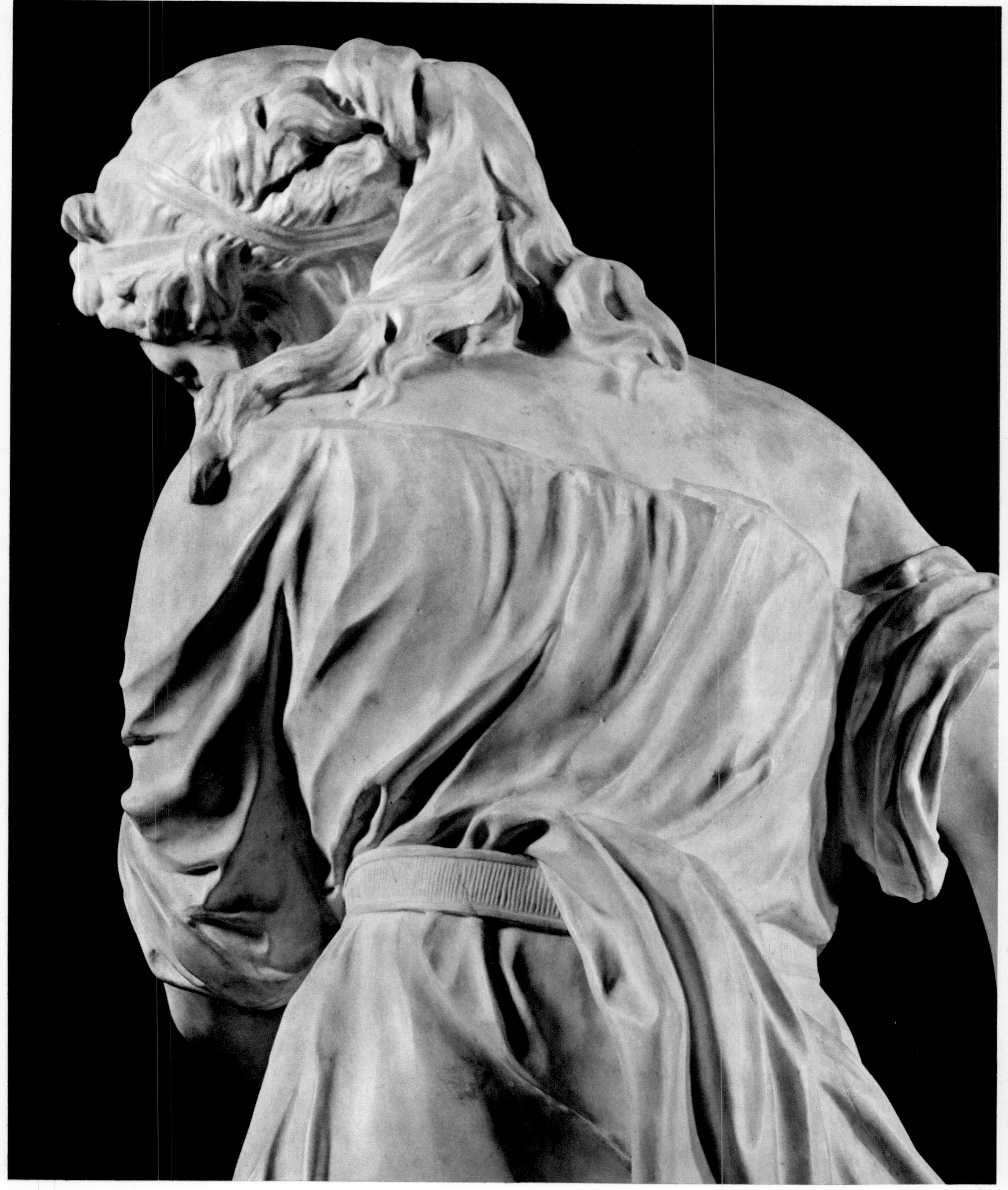

JEAN LOUIS LEMOYNE · *Diana,* Detail. See Page 154

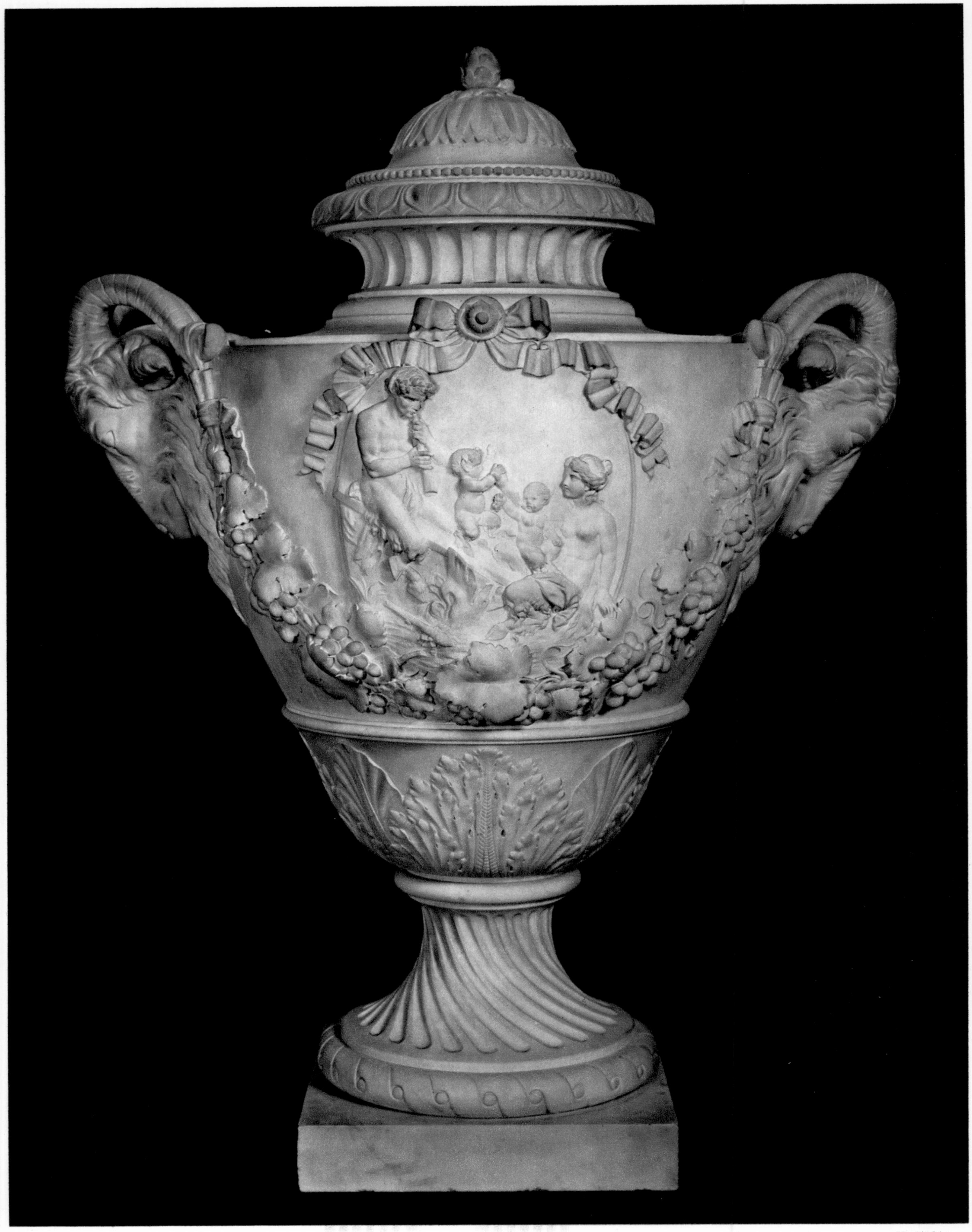

Marble H. 51¾ in.

CLODION · *Monumental Urn.* *Mellon Collection.* See Note 51

CLODION · *Monumental Urn,* Detail. See Page 158

JEAN ANTOINE HOUDON · *Alexandre Brongniard*, Detail. See Page 161

Marble H. 15 7/16 in.

JEAN ANTOINE HOUDON · *Alexandre Brongniard.* *Widener Collection.* See Notes 52, 53

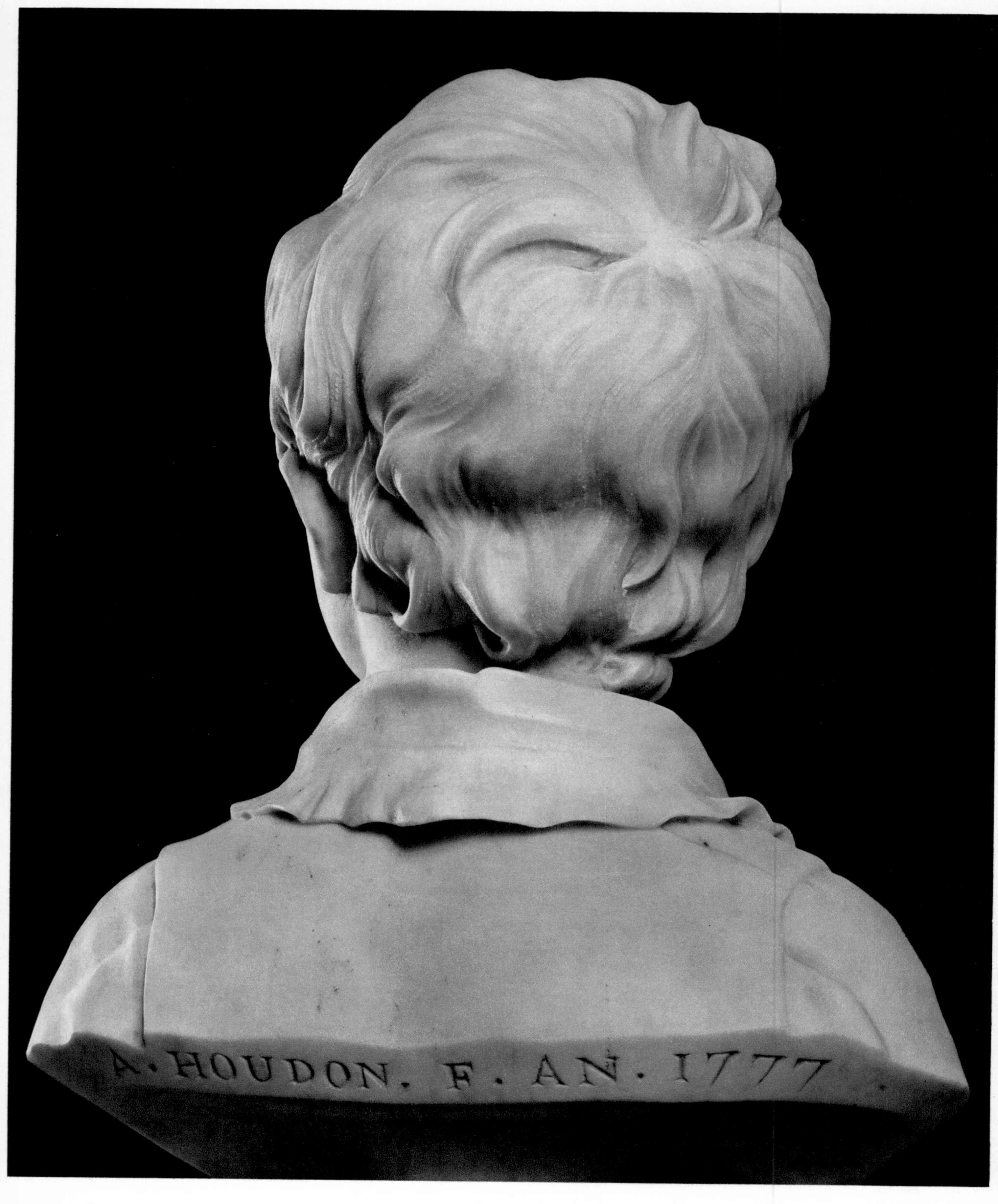

JEAN ANTOINE HOUDON · *Alexandre Brongniard,* Rear View. See Page 161

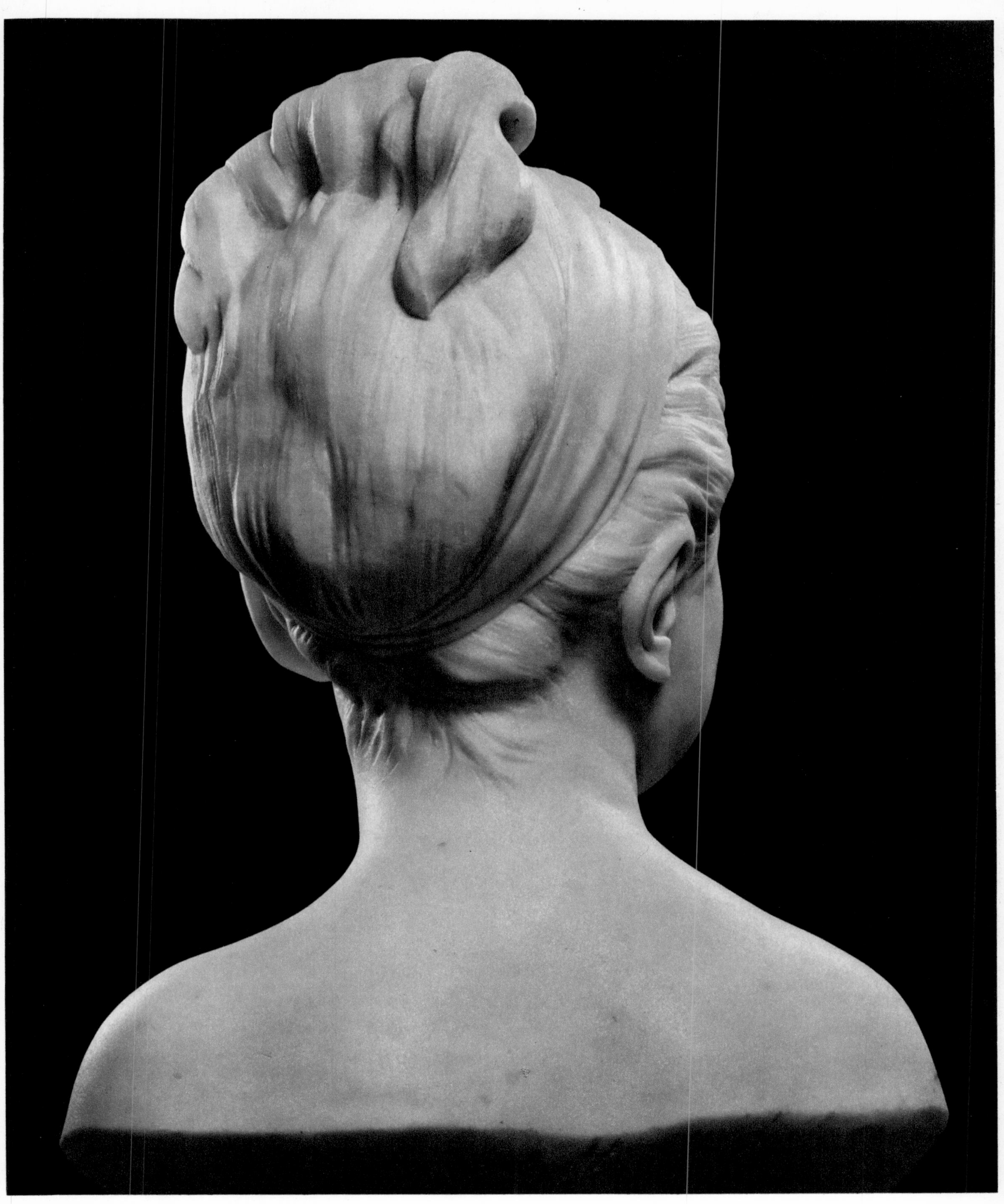

JEAN ANTOINE HOUDON · *Louise Brongniard,* Rear View. See Page 164

Marble

H. $14\frac{13}{16}$ in.

JEAN ANTOINE HOUDON · *Louise Brongniard.* *Widener Collection.* See Notes 52, 53

JEAN-BAPTISTE CARPEAUX · *Girl with a Shell*, Detail. See Page 167

Marble H. 36¼ in.

JEAN-BAPTISTE CARPEAUX · *Neapolitan Fisherboy.* *Kress Collection.* See Notes 54, 55

Marble H. 40¾ in.

JEAN-BAPTISTE CARPEAUX · *Girl with a Shell.* *Kress Collection.* See Notes 54, 55

Bronze

H. 41 in.

AUGUSTE RODIN · *The Age of Bronze.* *Simpson Collection.* See Note 56

NOTES ON THE PIECES ILLUSTRATED

NOTES ON THE PIECES ILLUSTRATED

These notes on each of the pieces illustrated are not intended to be exhaustive; they do not constitute a catalogue. Only a selection of pertinent bibliography is included, verbal descriptions are eliminated altogether, and the reasoning which deals with date or attribution is, in general, much abridged from the material available in the Gallery's catalogue files. For reference purposes the Gallery number of each piece is given directly after the title. Measurements are taken between points of greatest extension. They are given in inches for height, width (or length) and depth in that order. In the case of roundels or medals the diameter is given. Metric equivalents are added in parentheses.

1. FRENCH, c. 1140

MEDALLION ON THE CHALICE OF ABBOT SUGER OF ST.-DENIS. C-1. Page 27. Gold. H. 1¹⁄₁₆; W. 1 (0.03 x 0.024).

Collections: Abbey and Treasure of St.-Denis (to 1793); Bibliothèque Nationale, Paris; Towneley, England; Widener Collection.

The chalice with its Antique sardonyx (agate) cup, was described by Suger in his account of his administration of the Abbey and may be dated between 1135 and 1145 (when the account was written). Stolen from the Bibliothèque Nationale in 1804 and taken to England, the chalice disappeared for over a century. It was dramatically identified toward 1920 by comparison with a seventeenth-century drawing, and an early eighteenth-century engraving. Four of the five original gold medallions on the foot of the chalice were replaced in the seventeenth century, but the central medallion of Christ Pantocrator is still in place. Up to the present, scholars have not questioned the assumption that this repoussé medallion was made by a Western goldsmith in Suger's employ at St.-Denis. There is evidence that Suger was impressed by reports of works of Byzantine art; he could have brought back such a medallion from his Italian travels, or approved a design by a Western artist on a Byzantine model.

SELECTED REFERENCES: Suger, *De Rebus in administratione sua gestis*, ed. Panofsky (see below) p. 79; J. Guibert, *Les Dessins du Cabinet Peiresc au Cabinet des Estampes de la Bibliothèque Nationale*, Paris, 1910, pp. 27-46, pl. III; Félibien, *Histoire de l'Abbaye Royale de Saint Denys en France*, Paris, 1706, p. 541, pl. III R; M. Rosenberg, "Ein Wiedergefundener Kelch," *Festschrift zum Sechszigsten Geburtstag von Paul Clemen*, Bonn, 1926, pp. 209-217; E. Panofsky, *Abbot Suger on the Abbey Church of St.-Denis and its Art Treasures*, Princeton University Press, 1946, p. 205.

2. FRENCH, c. 1200

AQUAMANILE IN THE FORM OF A LION. C-5. Pages 28, 30. Bronze, with traces of gilt. H. 5⁷⁄₁₆; W. 6⅞; D. 2¾ (0.138 x 0.175 x 0.07).

Collections: Sigismond Bardac, Paris (sold 1913); Widener Collection.

This is a water-vessel, and as such is an excellent example of the closeness of sculpture to normal life in the Middle Ages—an aspect of sculpture which has been disappearing from our own lives of the twentieth century. The lion's open mouth is the spout for pouring water. The rounded, compact form of the animal makes it easy to grasp without a handle. The great majority, however, of vessels of this kind have handles. In the thirteenth and in the fourteenth centuries these handles are used artistically as linear motives repeating the curves of the animal, which gradually becomes more mannered and heraldic in design. In this example, remains of the ornamental and fantastic elements of the pre-Romanesque and Romanesque "animal style" are evident in the stylized head, the ornamental treatment of the braided hair on the back and incised ornamental delineation of the ribs. It is extremely hard to date such an example with certainty and to locate with equal certainty the workshop which produced it. The most reasonable approximation is Northeastern France, probably Lorraine, at the juncture of Romanesque and Gothic style toward 1200.

REFERENCE: O. von Falke and E. Meyer, *Bronzegeräte des Mittelalters*, Berlin, 1935, I, 62.

3. SIENESE, XV CENTURY

THE SHE-WOLF NOURISHING ROMULUS AND REMUS. A-155. Pages 29, 31. Bronze, dark, black-brown patina. H. 14⁵⁄₁₆; W. 25¼; D. 6¼ (0.38 x 0.642 x 0.159).

Collections: Said to have belonged to the collection of August the Strong, King of Poland, Elector of Saxony (c. 1730); Baron Wittinghof, Dresden (1826); Camillo Castiglioni, Vienna; Kress Collection.

A derivation from the well-known archaic bronze (generally considered Etruscan) now in the Museo del Campidoglio in Rome. The present example is somewhat smaller than the Antique *She-Wolf*, but it is an unusually large example among the various Renaissance bronze versions which go back to the Antique type for inspiration. It follows the archaic one very closely, but reveals differences of style, which can be traced in the mane, mouth and ears, and in the modeling of the flank. The casting is a magnificent example of craftsmanship. It may be dated after the middle of the fifteenth century. Renewed interest in the Antique bronze is shown by the fact that it was moved from the Lateran to the Capitoline hill in 1471.

The Roman She-Wolf was also the emblem of Siena. According to mythological tradition the city of Siena was founded by the sons of Remus, Senio and Aschio. The legend has it that when fleeing the persecutions of their uncle, Romulus, they found a refuge in the mountains where they founded Siena, thus providing the basis for later Sienese use of their family emblem—"The She-Wolf nourishing the twins." As early as the twelfth century the city of Siena was called "Vetusta" (very old). In 1204 a man who had dared to deride the She-Wolf was punished by the government.

The only example of comparable size in bronze is still in Siena on the marble column in front of the Palazzo Pubblico. The little figures of Romulus and Remus are later sixteenth-century additions; they follow closely the children added to the Capitoline example, which were made during the Renaissance.

SELECTED REFERENCES: L. Planiscig, *Collezione Camillo Castiglioni, catalogo dei bronzi*, Vienna, 1923, no. 10, and *Catalogue des bronzes antiques et de la renaissance de la Collection Camillo Castiglioni de Vienne*, Amsterdam, 1925, X.

4. ENGLISH (?), XIII CENTURY

AQUAMANILE IN THE FORM OF A HORSEMAN. C-4. Pages 32, 33. Bronze. H. 11³⁄₁₆; L. 14; D. 6 (0.285 x 0.355 x 0.153).

Collections: Sigismond Bardac, Paris (sold 1913); Widener Collection.

The top of the horseman's head is left open to receive water, the head and mouth of the horse forming the spout. The rider is apparently a huntsman and may have carried a falcon in his left hand (now missing, with the left arm). The piece appears to be a unique example; it is unusually large and there are no others known which are quite like it, although the theme and general characteristics of style exist in a fairly sizable number of examples. Opinion on the origin and date of this particular example has not yet crystallized. Von Falke considered it Eastern French of the late twelfth or early thirteenth century. It was considered to be Flemish, thirteenth century, while in the Widener Collection at Lynnewood Hall. The present attribution takes into consideration Scandinavian characteristics as well as those of the Continent. There is a possibility that the object might have originated in England where both Continental and Scandinavian elements of style could have fused.

Selected References: O. von Falke and E. Meyer, *Bronzegeräte des Mittelalters,* Berlin, 1935, I, 44; *Master Bronzes* (ed. G. B. Washburn), Albright Art Gallery, Buffalo, 1937, no. 113.

5. ENGLISH, LATE XIV OR EARLY XV CENTURY

Saint George and the Dragon. A-151. Pages 34-36. Brownish patined alabaster, with polychromy in red, gold, black and brown. H. 31 31/32; W. 23¾; D. 7 13/16 (0.812 x 0.603 x 0.198).

Collections: Said to have come from the Abbey Church of San Juan, Quejara, near Bilbao, Spain; Benoit Oppenheim, Berlin (1911); Otto H. Kahn, New York; Kress Collection.

This appears to be a unique piece, both for size and craftsmanship. Earlier theories that the group is Spanish or Franco-Flemish because it is of finer quality than the usual Nottingham shopwork do not seem tenable. That it originated in England is suggested by comparison with representations of the theme in English manuscripts of about 1400 (for example the *Beaufort Hours* in the British Museum). Details of the armor of this Saint find close parallels in late fourteenth and early fifteenth-century English tomb sculpture. Nelson (see below) has gone so far as to suggest that the group may have been carved for the center panel of the reredos of St. George's Chapel in Windsor (1367); his theory still remains to be tested thoroughly, but it is indicative of the extraordinary character and quality of the sculpture.

Selected References: E. Lüthgen, *Die abendländische Kunst des XV Jahrhunderts,* Bonn, 1920, p. 51; P. Nelson, in *The Archaeological Journal,* 1926, LXXXIII, 44-45; G. Swarzenski, *Arts of the Middle Ages,* Loan Exhibition, Museum of Fine Arts, Boston, 1940, p. 58.

6. PISANELLO. SCHOOL OF VERONA (c. 1395-1455)

Domenico Novello Malatesta. Page 37. Bronze. Diam. 3⅜; D. 9/32 (0.085 x 0.007). Reverse only illustrated, inscribed: OPVS PISANI PICTORIS ([by] Pisanello, painter).

Collections: Gustave Dreyfus, Paris; Kress Collection, Loan.

Domenico Novello Malatesta, younger brother of Sigismondo Malatesta, was Lord of Cesena (1429-1465). The very moving image of a knight kneeling before a crucifix may refer to Domenico Malatesta's vow to found the Hospital of the Holy Crucifix (fulfilled in 1452). The vow was made when he was pressed hard and near defeat in the battle of Montolmo in 1444. This interpretation is considered by Hill (see below) in dating the medal "probably about 1445."

Reference: G. F. Hill, *The Gustave Dreyfus Collection, Renaissance Medals,* Oxford, 1931, p. 14 (gives further references).

7-8. BURGUNDIAN, XIV CENTURY

Heraclius I. Page 38. Bronze. Diam. 3 27/32; D. 17/64 (0.097 x 0.006). Inscribed, obverse, around circumference: Name and titles of Heraclius in Greek. On the crescent: SVPER TENEB(R)AS NOSTRAS MILITABOR IN GENTIBUS. Across the field: AΠOΛINIS (possibly a corrupt form of Apollo) and ILLVMINA VVLTVM TVVM DEV' (possibly from: "Lord, lift Thou up the light of Thy countenance." Psalm 4.6). Reverse, around circumference: SVPER ASPIDEM ET BAZILISCUM . (Psalm 91.13: "Super aspidem et basiliscum ambulabis: et conculcabis leonem et draconem—Thou shalt tread upon the asp and the basilisk: the young lion and the dragon shalt thou trample under feet.") In the field, in Greek: "Glory to God in the highest and on earth peace, good will toward men." Luke 2.14.

Constantine the Great. Page 39. Bronze. Diam. 3¾; D. 21/64 (0.095 x 0.008). Inscribed: obverse, around circumference: CONSTANTINVS IN XPO DEO FIDELIS IMPERATOR ET MODERATOR ROMANORVM SEMPER AVGVSTVS. (Constantine faithful to the God-Christ and ever august Emperor-leader of the Romans). Reverse, around circumference: MIHI ABSIT GLORIARI NISI IN CRVCE DOMINI NOSTRI IHV . XPI . (Galatians 6. 14: "Mihi autem absit gloriari nisi in cruce Domini nostri Jesu Christi, per quem mihi mundus crucifixus est et ego mundo—But God forbid that I should glory save in the Cross of our Lord Jesus Christ, by whom the world is crucified unto me, and I unto the world.")

Collections: Gustave Dreyfus, Paris; Kress Collection, Loan.

These are castings, probably of the fifteenth century, of a series of medals in gold; the originals were made in France toward the end of the fourteenth century or very soon after 1400. Jean, Duc de Berry owned a number of such medals; Hill gives full credit to the record that a medal of Constantine and one of Heraclius were bought by him as early as 1402. The designs are consequently of great interest in the history of the medal. The strong religious emphasis and the complex play of texts and barbarous mixture of Greek and Latin used for inscriptions are medieval elements which were later to disappear in Renaissance medals. But the pictorial richness of design used in symbolism (see especially the reverses) was to prove a large part of the basis for the development which Pisanello and other Quattrocento Italian medallists brought about later. The reverse of the medal of Constantine symbolizes the Church and Paganism (the same scheme of a clothed and a naked woman was later used by Titian in a Neoplatonic context in his so-called "Sacred and Profane Love" as pointed out by Panofsky). The reverse of the Heraclius medal shows that Emperor bearing off the Cross which he recovered from the Persians and brought to Constantinople in 629. The theme of horses and chariot-cart was used by the Northern artist, Pol de Limbourg, in the calendar of the *Great Book of Hours* done for the Duc de Berry.

Reference: G. F. Hill, *The Gustave Dreyfus Collection, Renaissance Medals,* Oxford, 1931, p. 238 (gives other references).

9. FRENCH OR BURGUNDIAN, c. 1400

The Trinity. C-11. Pages 40-42. Morse or ecclesiastical clasp of gold and enamel. Diam. 5 (0.126).

Collections: Said to have belonged to Rodrigo Borgia, Pope Alexander VI; John Edward Taylor, London (sold 1912); Widener Collection.

Although there has been as yet no success in verifying the tradition that this morse belonged to Pope Alexander VI, the piece does appear to have been at one time in Italy, where it was probably brought (or sold) from France. Until recently the attribution was to Caradosso who worked in Milan about 1500. Both this curiously late date and the attribution to an Italian artist stem from an error which can be traced to its source in Molinier's classic work on medieval and Renaissance goldsmith-work *(Histoire des arts appliqués à l'industrie,* IV). There, the author did not distinguish sufficiently clearly between the earlier Northern work and later Italian Renaissance additions in the Gran "Crucifixion," which, with the famous "Golden Horse" of Altoetting, is a key-piece in the study of late fourteenth and early fifteenth-century gold-enamel work. Pieces in this technique and style are relatively rare today, but their importance, as highly-prized and easily portable objects, for the spread of what has been called the "International Style" is becoming better recognized. This object is among the finest examples of this art and appears to have been made at the peak of its development toward 1400, or soon after. The Valois Kings and Dukes favored particularly the creation of goldsmith-work in this style and technique and attracted, as they did their book illuminators, the artisans primarily from the Northern Mosan and Lower Rhenish regions.

Selected References: *Sales Catalogue of the J. E. Taylor Collection,* London (Christie's), 1912, no. 234; H. Kohlhaussen, in *Geschichte des Kunstgewerbes* (ed. H. T. Bossert), Berlin, 1932, V, 388 (there called the top of a reliquary); R. Krautheimer, in *The Art Bulletin,* XXIX, 1947, p. 31.

10. ENGLISH, XIV CENTURY

The Holy Trinity. A-150. Pages 43-45. Alabaster. H. 33[19]/32; W. 14; D. 11½ (0.991 x 0.335 x 0.292).

Collections: Alfredo Barsanti, Rome; Kress Collection.

This beautiful example of alabaster carving has been generally known for only a few years. In scale, quality of execution, and mixture of early and late Gothic style, it has already been recognized as very unusual, if not unique. The present attribution to an English master in the fourteenth century is supported from several details in analogy to English work. It must be recognized, however, that the statue does not reflect the mass-production style of the Nottingham School as it developed in the late fourteenth and fifteenth centuries. As far as is known, the piece was found in Paris, not in Rome; it had been suggested, but not proved by corroboratory evidence, that it is the same *Trinity* which is known to have been shipped from Southampton to Rome in 1382. Valentiner and Langton Douglas agree on the English origin of this extremely important piece. Georg Swarzenski has suggested that the hands, now missing, were probably originally of copper-gilt or silver, adding to the richness of effect provided by the glowing material of alabaster with polychrome accents (in part traceable today).

Selected References: R. Langton Douglas, in *Art in America,* 1943, pp. 203 ff.; W. R. Valentiner, *Origins of Modern Sculpture,* New York, 1946, p. 157.

11. UPPER RHENISH, c. 1440

The Dead Christ Supported by an Angel (The Trinity). A-144. Pages 46-48. Painted alabaster. Background and clouds, blue; roof-tiles, halos and angel's wings, red; traces of gilt on the rays of the angel's halo and hair. H. 12¼; W. 8[29]/32; D. 3⅞ (0.311 x 0.226 x 0.098).

Collections: J. and S. Goldschmidt, Frankfort-am-Main; Ralph Harman Booth, Detroit; Gift of Mrs. Ralph Harman Booth, in memory of her husband.

This is one of a family of rare reliefs from a workshop located by Georg Swarzenski on the Upper Rhine between Lake Constance and Bâle. Other examples are in the museums of Boston, Villingen, Freiburg-in-Baden, Sigmaringen and Zürich. The equally rare theme, a combination of the Trinity with the Man of Sorrows, is Franco-Burgundian in origin and traveled probably by portable goldsmith ware to the Rhine; an early example in gold and enamel (perhaps the first on record) is noted in the inventory of the Collection of the Duc de Berry toward 1400.

Selected References: G. Swarzenski, "Insinuationes Divinae Pietatis," in *Festschrift für Adolf Goldschmidt,* 1923, pp. 65 ff.; also in *Bulletin of the Museum of Fine Arts of Boston,* XLI, 1943, pp. 18 ff.

12. TINO DI CAMAINO, TUSCAN SCHOOL (Mentioned 1312-1337)

Madonna and Child with Queen Sancia, Saints and Angels. A-156. Pages 49-52. Alabaster. H. 20¼; W. 14⅞; D. 3⅜ (0.514 x 0.378 x 0.085).

Collections: Conte Alessandro Contini-Bonacossi, Rome; Henry Goldman, New York; Kress Collection.

Queen Sancia, the second wife of Robert the Wise of Anjou, King of Naples, retired to the Franciscan Order of the Poor Clares in 1343 after her husband's death. Before that time, however, she showed marked interest in the Franciscan Order to which she gave liberally; with her husband she might be called the founder of the Church of Santa Chiara in Naples; in 1334 she addressed the General Chapter of the Franciscans at Assisi as a "Mother of the Order." Like her husband, she would frequently wear, even before becoming a nun, the habit of the Order. She wears it here as she is shown kneeling, her crown on her wrist, with Saint Clara behind her at the left of the Virgin. She looks toward Saint Francis, who stands opposite her. The relief may have been the central panel of a devotional triptych and was probably commissioned by the Queen herself. A unique example of Tino's use of alabaster, it can be dated 1330-1335, when the artist was working on the altar in the Badia of Cava dei Tirreni and the tomb of Charles of Calabria in Santa Chiara, in Naples. The clarity and delicacy of the relief reveals some influence from French sculpture, an influence which may have been transmitted and reinforced by imported French ivories studied by Tino while he was working for the Angevin Court at Naples. The destruction and damage suffered by the royal tombs in Santa Chiara during World War II lend this relief additional value as a document for Tino's late style as well as for its historical importance.

Selected References: W. R. Valentiner, *Tino di Camaino,* Paris, 1935, pp. 115 ff., and *Catalogue, Exhibition of Italian Sculpture 1250-1500,* Detroit, 1938, no. 12; H. Keller, in Thieme-Becker, *Künstlerlexikon,* 1939, XXXIII, 186.

13. JACOPO DELLA QUERCIA. SIENESE SCHOOL (1367(?)-1438)

Madonna of Humility. A-157. Pages 53-56. Marble with

traces of gilt. H. 22 31/32; W. 19¼; D. 11⅛ (0.584 x 0.488 x 0.283).

Collections: Prince Ercolani, Bologna; Henry Goldman, New York; Kress Collection.

Medieval thought extolled humility as the "root" of Christian virtues and derived the word "humilitas" from "humus" (earth). Hence the chief element of the pose of the *Madonna of Humility,* presented as sitting on the ground and not upon a throne or as a standing figure. The theological, artistic and poetic implications of the theme are extremely rich (see M. Meiss, in *Art Bulletin,* XVII, 1936, pp. 435-464). Only in Italy, however, and in the Trecento did artists first sense the possibilities of their unity in a single image; and this seems to have occurred in Siena. In this case, painting appears to have preceded sculpture. The earliest known example in sculpture is, as stated by G. Swarzenski, the group presented here. It can be dated in the neighborhood of 1400 and represents as far as can be judged the early style of Jacopo della Quercia—before his existing work at Lucca and Ferrara and San Gimignano. This interpretation of date, so significant for our understanding of the origins of Quattrocento sculpture, is recent. For some years the piece was considered to be a product of Quercia's Bolognese or Sienese periods (after 1425) and at various times was held (without convincing reasons) to be the work of one of his later assistants or followers. As early as 1919, however, Planiscig expressed in a letter his opinion that it was by Quercia; this was also ultimately Valentiner's belief in 1940 (see below).

SELECTED REFERENCES: W. R. Valentiner, *Catalogue of the Henry Goldman Collection* (privately printed), 1922, No. 3; idem, in *Burlington Magazine,* March, 1940, p. 86; C. Seymour, Jr., and H. Swarzenski, in *Gazette des Beaux-Arts,* 1946, pp. 129-152 (give fuller references).

14. LORENZO GHIBERTI. FLORENTINE SCHOOL (1378-1455)

MADONNA AND CHILD. A-147. Pages 57, 58, 60. Painted terra cotta. Naturalistic flesh tones; mantle, gilt lined with blue; dress, gilt and red; hair, gilt. H. 40⅜; W. 24½; D. 11⅛ (1.025 x 0.622 x 0.283). Inscription on base in capitals: AVE MARIE • GRATIA • PLENA (Hail Mary, full of grace).

Collections: Said to have come from Santo Spirito, Florence; Eduard Simon, Berlin; Clarence H. Mackay, Roslyn, L. I., New York; Kress Collection.

Bode rightly called this relief the masterpiece of an important group of early Quattrocento half-length Madonnas in painted terra cotta and stucco. His attribution of the group was to Ghiberti and his school, and is the basis for the present attribution. Opinion, however, is still divided. The greatest scholar of Ghiberti's literary work, Schlosser, did not agree with Bode's attribution of the group to Ghiberti, and elements of Quercia's style have also been singled out and emphasized, in particular by Krautheimer. Planiscig ascribed this Madonna with two others in Berlin to Nanni di Bartolo (active 1419—before 1439); he was a collaborator with Donatello on the sculpture for the façade and Campanile of the Cathedral of Florence. Regardless of opinion as to authorship, however, this Madonna must be considered as a key-piece in the study of the interaction of several currents of style among terra-cotta sculptors in Florence during the second and third decades of the Quattrocento.

SELECTED REFERENCES: W. v. Bode, *Florentine Sculptors of the Renaissance,* New York, 1928, p. 66; L. Planiscig, Vienna *Jahrbuch,* N. F. IV, 1930, p. 82; R. Krautheimer, in *Parnassus,* VIII, Dec., 1936, p. 5; J. von Schlosser, *Leben und Meinungen des florentinischen Bildners Lorenzo Ghiberti,* Basel, 1941, p. 120.

15. DONATELLO, FLORENTINE SCHOOL (c. 1386-1466)

MADONNA AND CHILD. A-1. Pages 59, 61-63. Painted terra cotta. Naturalistic flesh tones, red dress, blue mantle lined with green, white veil with red and blue ornament. H. 47 9/16; W. 18 19/32; D. 13 3/16 (1.209 x 0.472 x 0.335).

Collections: Count Giacomo Michelozzi, Tavernelle; Henry Goldman, New York; Mellon Collection.

As in the case of the preceding piece (No. 14) there is today some difference of opinion as to attribution. Bode attributed this rare standing Madonna to Donatello. He was followed by Valentiner, who, however, more recently felt a mixture of styles which he thought might represent the work of a sculptor influenced both by Ghiberti and Donatello. He selected Michelozzo, but this attribution does not hold up in comparison with Michelozzo's known work. There are certain stylistic connections with Quercia (particularly in the head of the Virgin), and a number of motives such as the thumb-sucking child appearing as a kind of trade-mark in a group attributed by Bode to Ghiberti and his school (see No. 14). The analogies to Donatello's style are still sufficiently marked to warrant retaining Bode's attribution until more is known of the workshop or group of terra-cotta sculptors in Florence which combined in so striking a way the motives and styles of Donatello, Quercia and Ghiberti.

SELECTED REFERENCES: W. v. Bode, in *Kunst und Künstler,* XIX, 1921, pp. 238 ff; W. R. Valentiner, *Catalogue of the Henry Goldman Collection* (privately printed), 1922, No. 4, and in *The Art Quarterly,* III, 1940, pp. 196-200; G. Swarzenski in *Gazette des Beaux-Arts,* 1943, p. 287.

16. MICHELOZZO. FLORENTINE SCHOOL (c. 1396-1472)

MADONNA WITH THE SLEEPING CHILD. A-161. Pages 64, 65. White glazed terra cotta, with rounded base glazed in blue. H. 24⅜; W. 22 9/32; D. 8 7/16 (0.62 x 0.566 x 0.215). Originally a roundel (the blue background for the figures missing).

Collections: Charles Eliot Norton, Cambridge, Massachusetts, (probably acquired in Italy between 1830-1845); Quincy Shaw, Boston, Massachusetts; Kress Collection.

There is nothing in Luca della Robbia's known work which closely corresponds to the iconographic theme or the style of this relief. The connection with Luca is in the technique of glazed terra cotta. The style is much closer to Donatello, especially his second period (after 1425). But even here there are differences which cannot be reconciled: the direct and strong tridimensional effect of the relief and the lack of linear tension and mannered precision in drapery style do not recall Donatello's personal manner. We are led to an artist who was connected both with Luca della Robbia (technique) and Donatello (some elements of style). That this artist was Michelozzo is the hypothesis advanced at the present time. No other Florentine sculptor of any stature was working in terra cotta before 1450 except Luca della Robbia, Donatello and Michelozzo. And this relief in its naturalistic interpretation of a classical type in the head of the Madonna, the freedom of the drapery and wavy hair corresponds to the known work of Michelozzo more closely than to any other. A date after 1425, but not much after 1440, has been suggested for the relief.

REFERENCE: H. Swarzenski, in *Phoebus,* II, 1948, pp. 41-42.

17. DONATELLO

THE DAVID OF THE CASA MARTELLI. A-109. Pages 66-71. Marble. H. 64; W. 19¾; D. 16¹¹⁄₁₆ (1.625 x 0.502 x 0.424).

Collections: Roberto Martelli; Martelli family, Florence (from the fifteenth century to 1916); Widener Collection.

Vasari states that the Florentine banker, Roberto Martelli (an associate of Cosimo de' Medici), possessed marble statues of David and Saint John the Baptist by Donatello. This is the first definite mention in writing of the statue; it was, however, represented in the background of the portrait (Berlin) of Roberto's grandson, Ugolino Martelli by Bronzino (c. 1535), and is there shown as it may well have looked at the time in the courtyard of the palace. In 1802 the *David* was removed from the open courtyard to the interior of the palace.

Vasari's association of the *David* with the *Saint John the Baptist* (now in the Bargello) might reflect the fact that the statues were intended to be shown together as a pair. They are of almost exactly the same height and have in common the fact that they both represent forerunners of Christ and symbols of the city of Florence. It is possible that the recutting evident in the *David* may have resulted from a decision to bring its proportions closer to those of the slender *Saint John.*

The date of the statue is probably between Donatello's visit to Rome in 1433-1434 and 1440 when he began to abandon marble for bronze. Earlier as well as later dates have been suggested. But those suggested above correspond best with the classical influences evident especially in the head and with the drapery style similar to that of the Cantoria reliefs done for the Cathedral between 1433 and 1440. The statue was represented on a column in Botticelli's *Death of Lucretia* in the Gardner Museum, Boston. There are also three related statuettes in bronze (one in the Louvre, one in Berlin, and one in the collection of Sir Kenneth Clark) which are based on Donatello's design; although these have been claimed as casts from Donatello's original wax studies, they should probably be regarded as done rather freely after the marble.

SELECTED REFERENCES: Vasari, *Vite* (ed. Milanesi), II, 408; R. Borghini, *Il Riposo,* 1584, p. 320; W. v. Bode, *Denkmäler der Renaissance-Sculptur Toscanas,* Munich, 1892-1905, p. 24; Lord Balcarres, *Donatello,* London, 1903, pp. 52-54; P. Schubring, *Donatello (Klassiker der Kunst series),* Stuttgart, 1907, p. 38; A. Venturi, *Storia dell' arte italiana,* Milan, 1908, VI, 252; A. Marquand, in *Art in America,* IV, 1916, pp. 358 ff; W. R. Valentiner, in *Art News,* XXVI, 1928, pp. 15-21; H. Kauffmann, *Donatello,* Berlin, 1935, pp. 43-47; L. Planiscig, in *Phoebus,* II, 1949, pp.56-57 (rejects, on basis of photographs only, traditional attribution).

18. DONATELLO

SAINT JOHN THE BAPTIST. A-19. Pages 72, 73. Painted terra cotta. Olive-brown flesh tones, buff hair shirt, maroon mantle lined with green. H. 19¼; W. 20½; D. 10¼ (0.489 x 0.52 x 0.26).

Collections: Eugène Piot (1846), Charles Timbal, Gustave Dreyfus, Paris; Mellon Collection.

Generally dated about 1440, but it may perhaps have been executed a few years earlier. A far gayer but much overpainted stucco version belongs to the Kaiser Friedrich Museum in Berlin. The latter on a suggestion by Clarence Kennedy is now attributed to Desiderio da Settignano.

SELECTED REFERENCES: C. Perkins, in *Gazette des Beaux-Arts,* 1868 (2), p. 312, note 1; P. Vitry, in *Les Arts,* no. 72, 1907, pp. 9-10; W. v. Bode, *Florentine Sculptors of the Renaissance,* New York, 1928, p. 157; G. Swarzenski, in *Gazette des Beaux-Arts,* 1943, p. 288.

19. DESIDERIO DA SETTIGNANO. FLORENTINE SCHOOL (1428-1464)

THE CHRIST CHILD. A-148. Pages 74-76. Marble. H. 12; W. 10⁷⁄₁₆; D. 6⁷⁄₁₆ (0.305 x 0.265 x 0.163).

Collections: Oratory of San Francesco dei Vanchetoni, Florence (there mentioned, 1756); Kress Collection.

Studies of little children were extremely popular in Florence, especially in the second half of the Quattrocento, as the basis for representing the Young Christ Child and the Young Saint John the Baptist. They were either presented together in relief (recalling apocryphal legends of their meeting as children) or as companion busts. We know that this bust of a boy was intended to represent the Christ Child from the hole drilled in the crown of the head to attach a metal halo—a *Christ Child* by Antonio Rossellino in the Pierpont Morgan Library, New York, still preserves a halo. The present bust with one representing Saint John as a child, also in the Kress Collection (No. 21), stood in the Oratory of the Vanchetoni in Florence undisturbed for at least two centuries and perhaps more. Its traditional attribution to Donatello was changed to Desiderio toward 1900 and has been unchallenged since. The bust may be dated toward 1460. The quality of expression, between the outright laughter of the Benda Collection bust in Vienna and the more solemn *Bust of a Little Boy* from the Mellon Collection, has been recognized as one of the subtlest of Desiderio's achievements.

SELECTED REFERENCES: G. Richa, *Notizie istoriche delle chiese fiorentine,* IV, Florence, 1756, p. 92; F. Fantozzi, *Nuova guida . . . di Firenze,* Florence, 1842, p. 542; W. v. Bode, *Denkmäler,* Munich, 1892-1905, p. 104; M. Reymond, *La Sculpture florentine. Seconde moitié du XVe siècle,* Florence, 1899, pp. 70-71; W. v. Bode, *Florentine Sculptors of the Renaissance,* New York, 1928, p. 159; E. MacLagan, *Italian Sculpture of the Renaissance,* Harvard University Press, 1935, p. 136; L. Planiscig, *Desiderio da Settignano,* Vienna, 1942, p. 37.

20. DESIDERIO DA SETTIGNANO

BUST OF A LITTLE BOY. A-2. Pages 77-79. Marble. H. 10¹¹⁄₃₂; W. 9¾; D. 5⅞ (0.263 x 0.247 x 0.015).

Collections: Eugène Piot (acquired, Italy, 1848), Paul van Cuyck, Charles Timbal, Gustave Dreyfus, Paris; Mellon Collection.

Traditionally attributed to Donatello, this *Bust of a Little Boy* was correctly given to Desiderio by Bode and Reymond nearly half a century ago. The style of this bust in comparison with the Vanchetoni-Kress Collection *Christ Child* (see pages 74-76) is less impressionistic and closer to the children-putti of Desiderio's *Marsuppini Tomb* in Santa Croce, which can be dated c. 1455. There are, however, some elements which approach the style of the *Blessing Christ Child* of the San Lorenzo Tabernacle of 1461. The bust is accordingly dateable as between 1455 and 1460. It has always been a particular favorite in modern times. When Timbal sold his collection to Gustave Dreyfus, he found he was unable to part with this bust; an arrangement was made whereby he kept possession of it until he died, and it was actually only after his death that it entered the Dreyfus Collection.

SELECTED REFERENCES: E. Müntz, *La Renaissance en Italie et en France à l'époque de Charles VIII*, Paris, 1885, p. 171, and *Donatello*, Paris, 1885, p. 102; W. v. Bode, *Denkmäler*, Munich, 1892-1905, p. 97; M. Reymond, *La Sculpture florentine. Seconde moitié du XVe siècle*, Florence, 1899, p. 71; P. Vitry, in *Les Arts*, no. 72, 1907, pp. 6-8, 10; W. v. Bode, *Florentine Sculptors of the Renaissance*, New York, 1928, p. 158; L. Planiscig, *Desiderio da Settignano*, Vienna, 1942, pp. 29, 47.

21. ANTONIO ROSSELLINIO. FLORENTINE SCHOOL (1427-1478/9)

THE YOUNG SAINT JOHN THE BAPTIST. A-54. Pages 80, 81. Marble. H. 13⅝; W. 11¾; D. 6 11/32 (0.347 x 0.298 x 0.161).

Collections: Oratory of San Francesco dei Vanchetoni, Florence (there mentioned 1756); Kress Collection.

This bust stood with Desiderio's *Christ Child* (No. 19) in the Oratory of the Vanchetoni in Florence, and by the greatest good fortune the two are still together in their new places in the National Gallery of Art. Like the *Christ Child* it was traditionally ascribed to Donatello, but modern criticism has tended in general to give it to Antonio Rossellino. Planiscig has recently dated the bust toward the end of the artist's life between 1470 and 1475. The unusual quality of spirit, carried out with skillful atmospheric effects in the modeling, has always struck the imagination of critics. A. Venturi went so far as to suggest the inspiration of a very great genius: Leonardo.

SELECTED REFERENCES: G. Richa, *Notizie istoriche delle chiese fiorentine*, Florence, 1756, IV, 92; F. Fantozzi, *Nuova guida . . . di Firenze*, 1842, p. 542; W. v. Bode, *Denkmäler*, Munich, 1892-1905, p. 104, and *Die Sammlung Oscar Hainauer*, Berlin, 1897, p. 11; M. Reymond, *La Sculpture florentine. Seconde moitié du XVe siècle*, Florence, 1899, pp. 70-71; W. v. Bode, *Florentine Sculptors of the Renaissance*, New York, 1928, p. 159; H. Gottschalk, *Antonio Rossellino*, Berlin, 1930, p. 99; A. Venturi, *Storia dell' arte italiana*, Milan, 1935, X[1], 79; L. Planiscig, *Bernardo und Antonio Rossellino*, Vienna, 1942, pp. 38 ff., 57.

22. DESIDERIO DA SETTIGNANO

MARIETTA STROZZI. A-106. Pages 82-84. Marble. H. 22⅛; W. 20 15/32; D. 9⅝ (0.562 x 0.52 x 0.35). Unfinished. The nose and one shock of hair are restored.

Collections: Strozzi Family, Florence (until 1914); G. Magherini Graziani, Città di Castello; Widener Collection.

Vasari states that Desiderio made a marble portrait-bust of Marietta Strozzi, a member of the family of powerful bankers in Florence. She was born in 1448 and was thus only sixteen years old when Desiderio died. Whether this young lady appears more than sixteen years of age is a question which art historians may or may not be qualified to judge. The bust is reported, at all events, to have been found in the Strozzi palace, and might conceivably represent a version of Desiderio's Marietta. Another similar bust, also unfinished and from the Strozzi Palace, is in the Pierpont Morgan Library, in New York; it too has been called a portrait of Marietta, as has a finished bust in Berlin.

SELECTED REFERENCES: W. v. Bode, in *Amtliche Berichte der Berliner Museen*, 1914, XXXVI, 54, and *Florentine Sculptors of the Renaissance*, New York, 1928, p. 153; W. R. Valentiner, in *Art News*, XXVI, 1928, p. 16; E. MacLagan, *Italian Sculpture of the Renaissance*, Harvard University Press, 1935, p. 138; G. Swarzenski, in *Gazette des Beaux-Arts*, 1943, p. 290.

23. DESIDERIO DA SETTIGNANO

BUST OF A LADY. A-30. Pages 85, 86, 88. Marble. H. 20⅞; W. 19 13/16; D. 7 13/16 (0.53 x 0.488 x 0.199).

Collections: Alessandro Castellani, Rome; Arthur de Schickler, Martinvaast, France; Count Hubert de Pourtalès, Paris; Clarence H. Mackay, Roslyn, L. I., New York; Kress Collection.

This bust was for some time believed to be of Isotta da Rimini, one of the most brilliant women of the Renaissance. Comparisons with Matteo de' Pasti's medals which portray Isotta in profile do not bear out that identification. W. Suida (see below) has recently identified the features of the sitter with those of a lady generally thought to be Simonetta Cattaneo Vespucci, portrayed in Ghirlandaio's fresco of the *Madonna della Misericordia* in the church of Ognissanti, Florence (see H. Brockhaus, *Ricerche sopra alcuni capolavori d'arte fiorentina*, Milan, 1902). This interesting statement places additional value on the piece, since it would thus stand as the artistically highest and unique sculptural representation of the particular favorite of Giuliano de' Medici (see No. 35), and the ideal of feminine beauty in the last third of the fifteenth century in Florence.

The present bust has been called (by Valentiner) "one of the most perfect works, not only by Desiderio, but of the whole early Renaissance." No doubt, it shows a certain connection with Desiderio's busts of women in the Bargello and the Louvre; but, at the same time, it is stylistically more mature in the sense of the Florentine development. As a matter of fact, L. Planiscig (*Desiderio da Settignano*, Vienna, 1942) does not include this bust among Desiderio's works. Following Suida's identification of the sitter as Simonetta Vespucci (only eleven years old when Desiderio died), the attribution to Desiderio must be abandoned. Suida, pointing out the close stylistic connection with Verrocchio's circle, has suggested that the artist possibly might have been the young Leonardo. One can also think of Verrocchio himself, whose marble style may well have grown directly from Desiderio's.

SELECTED REFERENCES: W. v. Bode, in *Art in America*, XII, 1923, p. 5; W. R. Valentiner, *Catalogue of the Clarence H. Mackay Collection* (privately printed), 1926, no. 11; G. Swarzenski, in *Gazette des Beaux-Arts*, 1943, p. 290; W. Suida, in *The Art Quarterly*, XI, 1948, pp. 3-8 and XII, 1949, pp. 176-177.

24. FRANCESCO DA LAURANA. ITALIAN SCHOOL (c. 1425-1502)

A PRINCESS OF THE HOUSE OF ARAGON. A-8. Pages 87, 89, 90. Marble. H. 17 15/32; W. 17 25/32; D. 8 11/16 (0.444 x 0.452 x 0.221).

Collections: Alessandro Castellani, Rome (acquired before 1883 in Naples); Thomas Fortune Ryan, New York; Mellon Collection.

This bust can be dated about 1475 during Laurana's second stay at the Court of Naples (1472-1475). It is very similar to examples in the Frick Collection, New York, and in Berlin. The sitter has been variously identified with Beatrice of Aragon, her sister Eleanor, and Ippolita Sforza, wife of Alfonso II of Naples. The reliefs in the base symbolize in a general way the Neoplatonic concept of the struggle between virtue and unbridled passion (see E. Panofsky, *Studies in Iconology*, 1939, pp. 136 ff.)

Selected References: *Catalogue des objets d'art antiques du moyen-age et de la renaissance dépendant de la succession Alessandro Castellani,* Paris, 1884, No. 540; W. v. Bode, *Florentine Sculptors of the Renaissance,* New York, 1928, pp. 142-143; F. Burger, *Francesco Laurana,* Strassburg, 1907, pp. 130 ff.; W. Rolfs, *Franz Laurana,* Berlin, 1907, pp. 351 ff.; W. R. Valentiner, in *The Art Bulletin,* XIX, 1937, p. 509, in *The Art Quarterly,* I, 1938, p. 81, and V, 1942, pp. 287 ff. (reviewed by J. Pope-Hennessy, in *The Burlington Magazine,* 1943, p. 232); G. Swarzenski, in *Gazette des Beaux-Arts,* 1943, p. 301; R. Petrovitch, in *Gazette des Beaux-Arts,* 1947, pp. 78-79.

25. AGOSTINO DI DUCCIO. FLORENTINE SCHOOL (1418-after 1480)

Madonna and Child. A-5. Pages 91-94. Marble. H. 28; W. 22⅜ (0.71 x 0.568).

Collections: G. Brauer, Paris; J. Pierpont Morgan, New York; Mellon Collection.

Agostino di Duccio spent most of his life outside of Florence. One result was to spread the Florentine style into North Italy and Umbria. Another was to emancipate him from the stylistic development of sculpture in Florence itself and to lay the full burden of his own later development on himself. This may help to explain his unusual and very individual mannerism, but it also makes it difficult to reconstruct (without sure points of reference to the influence of other sculptors after 1442) the actual course of his style. The present relief has been dated as soon after Agostino's work at Modena in 1442; there is also a possibility that it may have been done during his stay in Perugia some fifteen years later. The frame of the relief is apparently the original; it is decorated by an Umbrian artist, probably Niccolò del Priore, a native of Perugia.

Selected References: H. Janson, in *The Art Bulletin,* XXIV, 1942, pp. 331, 334; G. Swarzenski, in *Gazette des Beaux-Arts,* 1943, p. 150.

26. MINO DA FIESOLE. FLORENTINE SCHOOL (1431-1484)

The Virgin Annunciate. A-46. Pages 95-97. Marble. H. 20; W. 14½; D. 5⅜ (0.51 x 0.368 x 0.136). Traces of inscription on base in Roman capitals: AVE MARIA GRATIA PLENA (see No. 14). Originally painted, at least in part.

Collections: Adriano de' Sani, Count Antonio Palmieri-Nuti, Siena; Clarence H. Mackay, Roslyn, L. I., New York; Kress Collection.

There are few examples of Renaissance sculpture which have so fascinated later eyes and minds as this. It was originally published in an engraving of the seventeenth century as a representation of Saint Catherine of Siena and was there ascribed, curiously enough, to Jacopo della Quercia. The costume is not the Dominican habit, however; and the inscription, which is still barely legible, indicates that the relief was really intended to represent the Virgin. The gentle inclination of the head would best fit the pose of the Virgin of the Annunciation, and it is possible that it once faced a similar bust of the Angel. The scales of modern scholarly opinion are tipped toward an attribution to Mino da Fiesole, who may have worked for a brief period in Siena. The haunting poetry of conception is reminiscent of Quattrocento Sienese painting. But the known sculpture of such Sienese painter-sculptors as Neroccio, Giovanni di Stefano, Francesco di Giorgio and Cozzarelli is quite different in style from our piece.

The importance and popularity of this image in Renaissance times is attested by a number of contemporaneous reproductions. Casts in painted stucco and terra cotta are preserved in the Metropolitan Museum of Art, New York; Rijksmuseum, Amsterdam; the Louvre. A marble variant attributed to the Sienese School is in the Museum of Lyon.

Selected References: L. Courajod, *Alexandre Lenoir, son Journal et le Musée des Monuments Français,* Paris, 1887, III, 362 ff.; C. Ricci, Catalogue, *Mostra d'antica arte senese,* Siena, 1904, no. 32; P. Schubring, *Die Plastik Sienas im Quattrocento,* Berlin, 1907, p. 148; A. Venturi, *Storia dell' arte italiana,* Milan, 1908, VI, 666; W. R. Valentiner in *Art in America,* XIII, 1925, pp. 253 ff.; and *Catalogue of the Clarence H. Mackay Collection* (privately printed), 1926, no. 16; L. Douglas in *The Burlington Magazine,* 1945, p. 223 (most recent summing up of evidence in favor of an attribution to Mino da Fiesole).

27-28 MINO DA FIESOLE

Charity. A-6. Pages 98, 100. Marble. H. 49¾; W. 17³⁄₁₆; D. 8⅝ (1.264 x 0.437 x 0.219).

Faith. A-7. Pages 98, 99, 101. Marble. H. 49¾; W. 17; D. 8⅜ (1.264 x 0.432 x 0.213).

Collections: Charles Timbal, Gustave Dreyfus, Paris; Mellon Collection.

These two figures must have originally been carved to decorate a tomb. According to tradition they came from the Church of Santa Maria Minerva in Rome, and Valentiner (see below) has suggested that they formed part of the tomb of Francesco Tornabuoni (died 1481) in that church. The style of the figures, however, is somewhat earlier and would appear to antedate the related figure of *Charity* on the tomb of Count Ugo of Andersberg in the Badia, Florence. This latter *Charity* was commissioned in 1469 and may well have been completed before Mino's departure for Rome in 1473. The work of Mino's last period in Rome, between 1473 and 1481, is more mannered and frequently shows the hands of assistants. The carving here is fresh and direct and represents Mino at his best—when he was combining the naturalism of Desiderio with his own feeling for stylized elegance.

Selected References: W. v. Bode, *Denkmäler,* Munich, 1892-1905, p. 126; D. Angeli, *Mino da Fiesole,* Florence, 1905, pp. 75-77; P. Vitry, in *Les Arts,* no. 72, 1907, pp. 16, 18 (resumes earlier opinions); W. R. Valentiner, in *The Art Quarterly,* VII, 1944, pp. 169, 177.

29. DESIDERIO DA SETTIGNANO

Saint Jerome in the Desert. A-107. Pages 102-105. Marble. H. 16¾; W. 21½ (0.427 x 0.547).

Collections: Karl Edward von Liphardt (who discovered the relief in Florence), Baron Renaud de Liphardt, Dorpat, Lithuania; Widener Collection.

The artistic richness and quality of this relief is reflected in the unusual array of suggestions as to its authorship. They range from Leonardo da Vinci, through Donatello and his school, Francesco di Giorgio, Pierino da Vinci, the "Master of the Tomb of Gian Antonio di Narni in San Antonio, Padua," to Desiderio. The last attribution seems by all odds the most likely today, and because of the strong influence of Donatello the work may be dated early in Desiderio's career, perhaps as early as 1450-1455. The design is a mine of cross-references between Florentine painting and sculpture. The unusual running figure to the right, for just one example, is similar to Castagno's *David* in the Widener Collection in the National Gallery of Art. Both derive from the motive of the so-called "Paedagogus" in Antique sculpture, available to the Quattrocento primarily in the Meleager cycle of Roman sarcophagus reliefs.

SELECTED REFERENCES: W. v. Bode, *Denkmäler,* Munich, 1892-1905, p. 95 (first puts forward the attribution to Desiderio); P. Schubring, *Donatello,* Stuttgart, 1907, p. 186; W. R. Valentiner, in *Art News,* XXVI, 1928, pp. 15-16; U. Middeldorf, in *Art in America,* XXVIII, 1940, pp. 28-29; L. Goldscheider, *Donatello,* Oxford-New York, 1941, p. 31 n.; G. Swarzenski, in *Gazette des Beaux-Arts,* 1943, p. 291 (suggests that the landscape may have been finished by Benedetto da Maiano); L. Planiscig, *Desiderio da Settignano,* Vienna, 1942, pp. 16, 42 (stresses early date).

30. FRANCESCO DI GIORGIO. SIENESE SCHOOL (1439-1502)

SAINT JEROME. Page 106. Bronze. H. 21⅝; W. 14$^{11}/_{16}$; D. 1$^{7}/_{16}$ (0.55 x 0.375 x 0.037).

Collections: Eugène Piot (until 1864), Gustave Dreyfus, Paris; Kress Collection, Loan.

The attribution of this relief has in the past been to Bertoldo. But there are un-Florentine elements of pictorial interest and handling in the background and above all in such details as the drapery of the figure which do not conform to Bertoldo's more severe and intellectual style. Comparison with both the painting and sculpture of Francesco di Giorgio makes clear a number of relationships in style and feeling and insistently suggests his own hand.

SELECTED REFERENCES: S. de Ricci, *The Gustave Dreyfus Collection, Renaissance Bronzes,* Oxford, 1931, p. 4 (gives previous references); A. S. Weller, *Francesco di Giorgio,* Chicago, 1943, pp. 162-163.

31. FRANCESCO DI GIORGIO

THE JUDGMENT OF PARIS. Page 107. Bronze, dark brown patina. H. 5⅝; W. 5$^{5}/_{32}$; D. $^{19}/_{64}$ (0.143 x 0.131 x 0.007).

Collections: Gustave Dreyfus, Paris; Kress Collection, Loan.

What one thinks about the attribution of this relief has an important bearing on one's whole concept of the history of Italian sculpture in the latter half of the Quattrocento. Bode first saw the relationship between this remarkable relief and several larger reliefs (in the Carmine, Venice; Victoria and Albert Museum, London—a version in Siena; Perugia Museum). He tended first to attribute the group as a whole to Verrocchio and then to Leonardo da Vinci while under Verrocchio's influence. It is clear, however, that one of the reliefs was made for Federigo da Montefeltro, Duke of Urbino, and comes from Urbino (where Verrocchio never worked and where Leonardo is not known to have come until 1502). It is also apparent that the style is close to the known sculpture of the rare Sienese genius, Francesco di Giorgio—who, significantly enough, worked for Federigo da Montefeltro in Urbino itself. The name of Francesco di Giorgio was first put forward as the author of the style of these reliefs by Schubring in 1907 and since that time the attribution has gained general support. The possibility of contact between Francesco di Giorgio and Leonardo in Florence suggested recently by Weller (see below) may explain the Leonardesque elements sensed by Bode. Our relief can be dated between 1475 and 1485 although the purpose of its making, or indeed whether it was actually done in Urbino, still remains mysterious.

SELECTED REFERENCES: W. v. Bode, in Berlin *Jahrbuch,* XXV, 1904, pp. 137-139; P. Schubring, *Die Plastik Sienas im Quattrocento,* Berlin, 1907, pp. 186-193, and *Die Italienische Plastik des Quattrocento,* Berlin, 1919, p. 190; S. de Ricci, *The Gustave Dreyfus Collection, Reliefs and Plaquettes,* Oxford, 1931, pp. 22-23 (reviews later attitudes on Bode-Schubring difference of opinion on attribution); A. S. Weller, *Francesco di Giorgio,* Chicago, 1943, pp. 161-162.

32. FRANCESCO DI GIORGIO

SAINT SEBASTIAN. Page 108. Bronze, black patina. Diam. 8; D. 1$^{5}/_{16}$ (0.203; 0.045).

Collections: Gustave Dreyfus, Paris; Kress Collection, Loan.

This roundel, with another representing Saint John the Baptist, in the Kress Collection, belongs to a group of four. A *Saint Anthony Abbot* belonging to the Liechtenstein Gallery in Vienna and a *Saint Jerome* belonging to the Kaiser Friedrich Museum of Berlin complete the series. All four seem to be by the same hand. Formerly attributed to the Paduan School, to Bellano, and then to Bertoldo, the reliefs now appear to be very probably by Francesco di Giorgio. Convincing reasons for the attribution on the basis of style have been given by Weller (see below). He suggests that the group of four reliefs may have originally been used for the decoration of a book cover or in connection with a cross or reliquary.

SELECTED REFERENCES: S. de Ricci, *The Gustave Dreyfus Collection, Reliefs and Plaquettes,* Oxford, 1931, p. 88; A. S. Weller, *Francesco di Giorgio,* Chicago, 1943, pp. 165-168.

33. MATTEO CIVITALE. TUSCAN SCHOOL (1436-1501)

SAINT SEBASTIAN. A-51. Pages 109, 110. Painted terra cotta. Light flesh tones, dark brown stump. H. 25⅝; W. 6$^{29}/_{32}$; D. 3$^{13}/_{16}$ (0.65 x 0.175 x 0.097). The figure was originally pierced with (metal?) arrows; they have disappeared and the holes have been filled.

Collections: Eugène Piot, Charles Timbal, Gustave Dreyfus, Paris; Kress Collection.

This statuette has been regarded as a model or small-scale variant of Civitale's life-size marble figure in the Cathedral of Lucca (executed between 1482 and 1484). But there are such differences in pose, proportions and expression between the two that Fabriczy and Schottmüller were unable to accept our statuette as by the same master. The real clue to the problem is that the celebrated Lucca statue is atypical of Civitale's style: it is severely influenced by Antonio Rossellino's *Saint Sebastian* of 1457 in Empoli. A terracotta *Saint Sebastian* given by Civitale to the Church of Monte San Quirico in 1497 is recorded, but is apparently no longer in existence. Our statuette may have been related to it. An Angel in the Metropolitan Museum of Art, New York, is stylistically close to our *Saint Sebastian* and supports the attribution.

SELECTED REFERENCES: C. Yriarte, *Matteo Civitale,* Paris, 1886, p. 58; P. Vitry, in *Les Arts,* 1907, no. 72, p. 18; C. v. Fabriczy, in Berlin *Jahrbuch,* XXX, 1909, p. 49; F. Schottmüller, in Thieme-Becker, *Künstlerlexikon,* VII, 1912, p. 26; W. R. Valentiner, *Catalogue, Exhibition of Italian Sculpture,* Detroit, 1938, no. 78; G. Swarzenski, in *Gazette des Beaux-Arts,* 1943, p. 299.

34. ANDREA DEL VERROCCHIO. FLORENTINE SCHOOL (1435-1488)

PUTTO POISED ON A GLOBE. A-17. Pages 111, 112. Terra

cotta covered with putty-colored paint. H. 29½; W. 15; D. 11$^{13}/_{16}$ (0.75 x 0.381 x 0.30).

Collections: Charles Timbal, Gustave Dreyfus, Paris; Mellon Collection.

The prototype of this figure is the running Eros theme of classical Antiquity. But exactly what it was intended for when it was modeled by Verrocchio is uncertain. The most generally held assumption is that it is a model for a bronze fountain figure; there are unquestionable relations with the bronze *Winged Boy with a Dolphin* (Palazzo Vecchio, Florence) which Verrocchio modeled and cast for the Medici in 1476, and a *Mercury on a Globe* executed for a fountain in 1515 by Rustici, who was one of Verrocchio's followers in Florence and might well have carried out the idea which Verrocchio never was able to put into permanent form. Our putto is quite a bit later in style than the *Boy with a Dolphin* and might possibly be connected with the fountain figure which Verrocchio was commissioned, just before his death, to do for Matthias Corvinus of Hungary. Maud Cruttwell (see below) advanced the theory that it might be connected with the lost putto which Vasari states Verrocchio designed for the clock of the New Market Place of Florence; in this case the outstretched arm might have been intended to hold a hammer to strike the hour. In style the figure is related to the Christ Child of Verrocchio's terra-cotta *Madonna of Santa Maria Nuova* (Bargello) and to drawings of children on a page of Verrocchio's studies in the Louvre.

Selected References: C. Ephrussi, in *Gazette des Beaux-Arts,* 1879, p. 311; W. v. Bode, *Denkmäler,* Munich, 1892-1905, p. 142; H. Mackowsky, *Verrocchio,* Leipzig, 1901, p. 38; M. Cruttwell, *Verrocchio,* London, 1904, p. 70; P. Vitry, in *Les Arts,* no. 72, 1907, p. 24; A. Venturi, in *L'Arte* XXVIII, 1925, p. 146; B. Wiles, *The Fountains of Florentine Sculptors and Their Followers from Donatello to Bernini,* Harvard University Press, 1933, p. 9.

35. ANDREA DEL VERROCCHIO

Giuliano de' Medici (1453-1478). A-16. Pages 113-116. Terra cotta, painted brown, waxed, probably originally polychromed. H. 24; W. 26; D. 11⅛ (0.61 x 0.66 x 0.283).

Collections: Eugène Piot (1846), Charles Timbal, Gustave Dreyfus, Paris; Mellon Collection.

In 1478 Giuliano de' Medici, the handsome younger brother of Lorenzo the Magnificent, was assassinated in the Cathedral of Florence, while attending Mass; this was the opening gambit of the Pazzi Rebellion. Few events shook Florence more than this uprising, and Giuliano, who was the idol of the Florentines in life, became something of a martyr in death. His likeness appeared in a great number of memorial medals and painted portraits. The spirit of this bust is very different from the known memorial portraits, and this suggests strongly that it is a likeness from life. It may have been done as a commemoration of the famous tournament of 1475 which Giuliano gave in honor of Simonetta Vespucci. Verrocchio is known to have designed some of the decor of the tournament, and may also have designed the armor worn by Giuliano on that occasion.

Selected References: *Le Magasin pittoresque,* no. 34, 1866, p. 41; W. v. Bode, *Denkmäler,* Munich, 1892-1905, p. 142; H. Mackowsky, *Verrocchio,* Leipzig, 1901, p. 42; M. Cruttwell, *Verrocchio,* London, 1904, p. 88; P. Vitry, in *Les Arts,* no. 72, 1907, p. 22; T. Trapesnikoff, *Porträtdarstellungen der Mediceer des XV Jahrhunderts,* Strassburg, 1909, pp. 68 ff.; G. Swarzenski, in *Gazette des Beaux-Arts,* 1943, p. 298.

36. ANDREA DEL VERROCCHIO

Lorenzo de' Medici (1449-1492). A-146. Pages 117-119. Painted terra cotta. Brown flesh tones, black gown, red undergarment, dark red headdress. H. 25⅞; W. 23¼; D. 12⅞ (0.658 x 0.59 x 0.328).

Collections: Emilio Santarelli, Florence; E. Nicholl Dennys, Henry Labouchere, Lord Taunton, London (by 1850); Edward A. Vessey Stanley, Bridgewater, England; Clarence H. Mackay, Roslyn, L. I., New York; Kress Collection.

The purpose of this bust was probably political. It represents Lorenzo after his successful weathering of the Pazzi Rebellion and his bold trip to Naples when his diplomacy, involving most of Europe, gave to Florence a short-lived security. The burger's costume is an important feature of Medicean policy of the fifteenth century—it suggests the democratic flavor which the family attempted with some success to attach to their control of the city-state. The grim features are a warning to enemies and plotters to keep within bounds.

The bust is the finest of several versions and close variants (examples in Berlin, Forlì). It does not appear to have been done from Lorenzo's death mask (1492), and may well be the closest to the example which a drawing by Leonardo (Windsor, 12442R) suggests was in Verrocchio's workshop before 1483. It must date, however, after 1480, and corresponds in its forceful presentation of a leader to Verrocchio's conception of Colleone—his last known work before his death in 1488. Interestingly enough, the bust was first exhibited in the nineteenth century as by Michelangelo.

Selected References: *Catalogue of Works of Ancient and Medieval Art Exhibited at the House of the Society of Arts,* London, 1850, no. 617; J. C. Robinson, *Catalogue of the Special Loan Exhibition of Works of Art,* London (South Kensington Museum), 1862-1864, no. 1; Trapesnikoff, *Portratdärstellungen der Mediceer des XV Jahrhunderts,* Strassburg, 1909, p. 50; W. v. Bode, in *Art in America,* XII, 1923, p. 5; W. R. Valentiner, *Catalogue of the Clarence H. Mackay Collection* (privately printed), 1926, p. 9 ff., and in *Art in America,* XXIII, 1933, pp. 249 ff.

37. GIOVANNI ANTONIO AMADEO. LOMBARD SCHOOL (1477-1522)

Lodovico Sforza, called Il Moro. A-9. Page 120. Marble. Diam. 24; D. 2 (0.61; 0.051). Inscription in Roman capitals in circumference: • LUDOVICUS • M. SF. DVX. BARI. (Lodovico Maria Sforza, Duke of Bari).

Collections: John Charles Robinson, London; Charles Timbal, Gustave Dreyfus, Paris; Mellon Collection.

Lodovico Il Moro was able to attract to his court, and to hold during his reign in Milan, the two greatest artists of his generation: Bramante and Leonardo. This relief is related in style to Amadeo's Sforza medallion portraits which are still in place in the famous Certosa (Carthusian Monastery) at Pavia. These are believed to have been done in 1491-1492. The present relief was probably not executed before that time and almost certainly was not begun after 1494; for in that year Lodovico added the Duchy of Milan to his title and this would have appeared in the inscription. A pendant representing his nephew, Gian Galeazzo Sforza, to whom he succeeded as Duke of Milan, is also in the National Gallery of Art (No. A-10). A medal by Caradosso and several silver coins may have been the basis for the designs of both portraits. A related roundel in the Louvre (no. 649).

Selected References: *Le Magasin pittoresque,* no. 33, 1865, p. 333; P. Vitry, in *Les Arts,* no. 72, 1907, pp. 29, 32; F. Malaguzzi Valeri, *La Corte di Lodovico il Moro, la vita privata,* Milan, 1913, p. 36, and *Giovanni Antonio Amadeo,* Bergamo, 1904, p. 319; G. Clausse, *Les Sforza et les arts en Milanais,* Paris, 1909, p. 180; G. Swarzenski, in *Gazette des Beaux-Arts,* 1943, p. 300.

38. ATTRIBUTED TO ALBERTI. FLORENTINE SCHOOL (1404-1472)

Leone Battista Alberti. Page 121. Bronze, black patina. H. 7²⁹⁄₃₂; W. 5¹¹⁄₃₂; D. ⅝ (0.201 x 0.136 x 0.015). Inscribed: • L • BAP • (Leo Baptista, the stops shaped like eyes).

Collections: Vicomte de Janzé, Charles Timbal, Gustave Dreyfus, Paris; Kress Collection, Loan.

Ascribed by Hill to Alberti, who is known to have been interested enough in sculpture to have written a book "De Statua" *(Breve compendium de componenda statua).* According to Hill, the plaque may be dated very early: about 1435. The shape of the plaque with the placing of the profile recalls an Antique gem. The device of the winged (and apparently dissected) eye is generally thought to refer to Alberti's interest in optics and the application of optics to representation in painting. A smaller plaque similar to the present example is in the Louvre; this one, however, is "easily the finer of the two" (Hill). The example in the Armand-Valton Collection in the Bibliothèque Nationale, Paris, is generally considered an after-cast.

Selected References: G. F. Hill, *Medals of the Renaissance,* Oxford, 1920, p. 46; S. de Ricci, *The Gustave Dreyfus Collection, Reliefs and Plaquettes,* Oxford, 1931, p. 2 (gives further references).

39. CRISTOFORO SOLARI. LOMBARD SCHOOL (c. 1460-1527)

Madonna and Child. A-158. Pages 122, 123. Marble. H. 19¾; W. 22 (0.502 x 0.560).

Collections: Otto H. Kahn, New York; Kress Collection.

To be dated in the last quarter of the fifteenth century, possibly during the sculptor's documented stay in Venice in 1489. The composition and iconography are to be found previously in Venetian painting. The Virgin recalls the Venetian period of Andrea Solari (or Solario), the elder brother of Cristoforo, who may have been his teacher. The motive of the Virgin with the Sleeping Child may be interpreted as an analogy to the more frequently seen "Pietà" (in which the Virgin holds the dead Christ on her lap); in this case the meditation of the Madonna on the future death of her Son is not only suggested by the inert pose of the Child, but by the relief in the background which shows the three Holy Women on their way to the Sepulcher, led, curiously, by the Christ Child. An earlier Florentine version of the theme is given in No. 16, plates 38-39.

Reference: H. Swarzenski, in *Phoebus,* II, 1948, pp. 39-40.

40. PIETRO LOMBARDO. LOMBARD - VENETIAN SCHOOL (c. 1435-1515)

A Singing Angel. A-47. Pages 124-126. Marble. H. 33⅞; W. 11; D. 11²⁷⁄₃₂ (0.86 x 0.28 x 0.30).

Collections: Chabrière-Arles, Lyon; Clarence H. Mackay, Roslyn, L. I., New York; Kress Collection.

This was probably one of a pair of angels which stood on the summit of a tomb, like that of Pietro Lombardo's monument to Pietro Mocenigo in SS. Giovanni e Paolo, Venice (1476-1480). The marked resemblance of this angel with those on the Mocenigo monument is the basis for the attribution to Pietro Lombardo and for a dating of about 1480. The angel was at one time attributed to Amadeo.

Selected References: G. Migeon, in *Les Arts,* no. 39, 1905, p. 10; W. R. Valentiner, in *Art in America,* XV, 1925, p. 219; and *Catalogue of the Clarence H. Mackay Collection* (privately printed), 1926, no. 18; G. Swarzenski, in *Gazette des Beaux-Arts,* 1943, p. 301.

41. JACOPO SANSOVINO. FLORENTINE-VENETIAN SCHOOL (1486-1570)

Venus Anadyomene. A-21. Pages 127-129. Bronze. H. 65⅞; W. 18½; D. 13¼ (1.673 x 0.47 x 0.337).

Collections: Said to have been in the collection of Duke Antonio Litta Visconti Arese, Milan; Mobilier du Palais-Royal (after 1797); Prince Napoleon, Palais-Royal, Paris (sold 1872); George J. Gould, Lakewood, New Jersey; Mellon Collection.

This statue, a rare example in American collections of large-scale Renaissance bronze casting, is attributed to Jacopo Sansovino for reasons of style. It would appear to be fairly early, certainly not much later than 1525, and represents a moment in his career when he was most plainly influenced by classical sculpture. The statue is known to have come from North Italy. A letter of Pietro Aretino of 1527 or 1528 mentions a statue of Venus which Sansovino was commissioned to make for Mantua; there was also a *Venus* by Sansovino in the Palazzo Giusti, Verona. These references, while they cannot be proved as connected with our statue, corroborate in a general way the stylistic evidence for the attribution to Sansovino.

The exact provenance of the statue is unknown, although there is an unverified record that it was at one time in Milan. It is known, however, that it was brought to Paris by Napoleon with a great number of works of art selected from Milan, Tortona, Bologna, Verona and other North Italian cities as "war indemnity" according to terms of the Treaty of Campo Formio in 1797. Placed in the Palais-Royal (it bears the inventory number 6316) it remained there until 1872, having escaped the fire in the Palace during the Commune. A report states that it was saved by being thrown out of a window. Whether this is true or not, the bronze shows little evidence of damage, but lacks at present a dolphin which was at one time attached to the base behind Venus's left foot.

Reference: *Sales Catalogue of the Collection of Prince Napoleon* (Christie's), London, 1872.

42. ANDREA RICCIO. PADUAN SCHOOL (1470-1532)

The Entombment. Pages 130-132. Bronze. H. 19¹³⁄₁₆; W. 29¹¹⁄₁₆; D. 3¼ (0.504 x 0.75 x 0.082). Inscribed on jar carried by a bearded man: AERDNA (reverse of Andrea).

Collections: Gustave Dreyfus, Paris; Kress Collection, Loan.

In 1581, Francesco Sansovino, author of an early guide to Venice, described in the church of the Servi an altar dedicated to the Holy Cross, which was decorated with five "very beautiful" compositions in bronze. Four plaques by Riccio treating the story of the Cross are now in the Museo Archeologico, Venice. They have been identified as coming from that altar. This extraordinary relief was called by Seymour de Ricci (see below) the missing fifth plaque. Planiscig has pointed out very close relations with the Servi altar plaques, but did not consider the present relief as originally part of the ensemble. He placed this relief stylistically a little later than the Servi series. And it would appear that in design and plasticity it marks an advance. The question of its original position as part of the altar decoration, however, is still open; conceivably this relief, somewhat larger than the other four, might have been the central panel, finished after, rather than before, the others.

No other bronze relief by Riccio, comparable in size or quality, has come to this country. It may be dated between 1500 and 1510, just before the artist's monumental Paschal candle-holder in Padua; the *Entombment* on this latter bronze has many details in common with the relief from the Kress Collection.

Selected References: L. Planiscig, *Venezianische Bildhauer der Renaissance,* Vienna, 1921, pp. 125-126, and *Andrea Riccio,* Vienna, 1927, pp. 211-220 (treats whole problem of Servi reliefs); S. de Ricci, *The Gustave Dreyfus Collection, Renaissance Bronzes,* Oxford, 1931, p. 2.

43. FRANCESCO DA SANT'AGATA. PADUAN SCHOOL (active c. 1520)

Hercules and Antaeus. A-113. Pages 133-135. Bronze, dark patina. H. 15¹⁄₁₆; W. 4¾; D. 10½ (0.38 x 0.12 x 0.265).

Collections: Madame Louis Stern, Paris; Widener Collection.

Done about 1520-1530, the composition is derived from Antique sculpture (an example is the *Hercules and Antaeus* of the Pitti Palace) and the same motive, treated with very different emphasis, was used earlier in the Renaissance by Antonio Pollaiuolo in his small bronze group in the Bargello. Although fairly recently the attribution of our group to Francesco da Sant'Agata has been questioned (see below), it is difficult to give the piece to any other artist except the sculptor we know by that name. He is a mysterious figure—identified through only one sixteenth-century reference and one piece (a boxwood *Hercules* in the Wallace Collection, London) which carries a signature believed to be his. On this slender foundation of fact have been grouped a number of bronzes which have in common characteristics of graceful proportions and a particular expression of movement. This group is the only one of these pieces which combines two figures. The Hercules is reminiscent in several details of the Wallace *Hercules* and its bronze variant in the Ashmolean Museum, Oxford. The Antaeus appears as a single figure in a bronze now in Detroit and is closely related to the walking "Niobid" in the Wallace Collection and similar figures in the Louvre and formerly in Braunschweig—all generally attributed to Francesco da Sant'Agata.

Selected References: W. v. Bode, *Die italienischen Bronzestatuetten der Renaissance,* Berlin, 1907, I, p. 42; C. Dreyfus, in *Les Arts,* no. 119, 1911, pp. 10, 12; L. Planiscig, *Venezianische Bildhauer der Renaissance,* Vienna, 1921, p. 302, also *Andrea Riccio,* Vienna, 1927, p. 222 (there tentatively attributed to Gambello); *Master Bronzes* (ed. G. B. Washburn), Albright Art Gallery, Buffalo, 1937, no. 139 (as by Francesco da Sant'Agata).

44. VINCENZO DANTI. FLORENTINE - UMBRIAN SCHOOL (1530-1576)

The Descent from the Cross. A-105. Pages 136-138. Bronze, black lacquer patina. H. 17½; W. 18½ (0.445 x 0.47).

Collections: Bardini, Florence; Hainauer, Berlin; Widener Collection.

The attribution to Vincenzo Danti is based on the close resemblance in style to his well-known reliefs: the *Serpent of Bronze* and the *Sportello* now in the Bargello. These are believed to have been done for Cosimo I, Duke of Tuscany in 1560-61, when Danti was in Florence. This relief must date from about the same time and was probably done in Florence. It is more interesting from a technical point of view than the Bargello examples since it shows practically no retouching or chasing after the cast (in the lost-wax process) was made.

Selected References: W. v. Bode, *Die Sammlung Oscar Hainauer,* Berlin, 1897, pp. 22, 79; W. R. Valentiner, in *Art News,* XXVI, 1928, p. 21.

45. ANNIBALE FONTANA. LOMBARD SCHOOL (1540-1587)

The Adoration of the Shepherds. A-23. Pages 139-141. Terra cotta. H. 43; W. 22¾ (1.092 x 0.578).

Collections: Trivulzio, Milan; Kress Collection.

This is the original model for the central relief in marble done for the façade of Santa Maria presso San Celso in Milan. Annibale Fontana was paid for the marble *Adoration* on July 8, 1580. This terra cotta can be dated a little before that time. The façade sculptures for Santa Maria presso San Celso occupied Fontana for some years. They are among the most prominent specimens of Italian, and especially Lombard, sculpture in the last third of the Cinquecento.

Selected References: S. Vigezzi, *La scultura lombarda nel cinquecento,* Milan, 1929, pp. 97-106; E. Kris, in *Mitteilungen des kunsthistorischen Institutes in Florenz,* III, 1930, pp. 201-253; E. F. Bange, *Berliner Museen: Berichte,* LII, 1931, pp. 50-51; A. Venturi, *Storia dell' arte italiana,* 1937, X³, 472.

46. GIOVANNI BOLOGNA. FLEMISH-FLORENTINE SCHOOL (1524-1608)

Mercury. A-20. Pages 142-145. Bronze, dark brown patina. H. 69⅝ (including head of wind-god, but not circular base); W. 19²³⁄₃₂; D. 37⁵⁄₁₆ (1.77 x 0.485 x 0.949).

Collections: Stroganoff, Rome (acquired in Italy before 1800); Sir George Donaldson, London; Henry E. Huntington, San Marino, California; Mellon Collection.

This is a fine version of the famous *Mercury* of which the first cast is generally considered to be the bronze now in the Bargello. There are obvious differences in detail and proportions which indicate that the two are not from the same model; nor is this an after-cast from the Bargello piece. The date of this example is uncertain, but could be prior to 1600. It is possible that it is connected with a replacement of the first Medici cast, removed to Rome from the Accaiuoli Gardens in Florence in 1598. A late source records a tradition that Giovanni Bologna made such a replacement. The style suggests a close follower: Adrien de Vries (see page 149).

Selected References: Baldinucci, *Notizie de'professori del disegno,* Florence, 1688, IV, 128; A. Desjardins, *La Vie et l'oeuvre de Jean Bologne,* Paris, 1883, pp. 31-32, 61-65; J. Dupail, *Le Mercure volant,* London (privately printed), 1904, *passim;* G. Swarzenski, in *Gazette des Beaux-Arts,* 1943, pp. 302-303.

47. BENVENUTO CELLINI. FLORENTINE SCHOOL (1500-1571)

VIRTUE OVERCOMING VICE. A-101. Pages 146, 148. Bronze, black lacquer patina. H. 9⁹⁄₁₆; W. 6⅞; D. 3½ (0.243 x 0.175 x 0.09).

Collections: John Edward Taylor, London (sold 1912); Widener Collection.

The composition was apparently one of the most popular of all sixteenth-century small-bronzes, and appears in a number of variants. In some of these the figure of Vice appears alone (Victoria and Albert Museum, London), and in some Vice is represented as a woman rather than a man (formerly Palazzo Borghese, Rome and before the last war in the Alphonse de Rothschild Collection, Vienna). Among the groups similar to this one are examples in the Frick Collection, New York (formerly in the J. P. Morgan Collection); in Berlin (before World War II) and in the Victoria and Albert Museum, London (Webb Fund, 1929). The example formerly in the Palazzo Borghese forms the top of an inkstand. The relationships of all these versions and variants have not been thoroughly worked out. The attribution of the design to Cellini is due to Bode, and has been generally accepted on stylistic grounds in lieu of any documentary evidence, which is strangely lacking. It is altogether probable that the artist was another Florentine Mannerist: Pierino da Vinci (Planiscig's attribution) or possibly Domenico Poggini (for whose style see U. Middeldorf, in *Burlington Magazine,* LIII, 1928, pp. 9-17; several bronzes of related style in the Huntington Library and Art Gallery, San Marino, are attributed tentatively to Poggini).

SELECTED REFERENCES: *Sales Catalogue of the J. E. Taylor Collection* (Christie's), London, 1912, no. 26; L. Planiscig, *Piccoli bronzi italiani del rinascimento,* Milan, 1930, pp. 43-45 (for other versions and general problem); *Master Bronzes* (ed. G. B. Washburn), Albright Art Gallery, Buffalo, 1937, no. 138.

48. ADRIAEN DE VRIES. DUTCH-FLORENTINE SCHOOL (c. 1560-1627)

VIRTUE AND VICE. A-141. Pages 147, 149-151. Bronze, light brownish patina. H. 30⁷⁄₁₆; W. 13¹¹⁄₁₆; D. 12½ (0.773 x 0.348 x 0.318). Signed on base: ADRIANVS FRIES FE 1610.

Collections: Said to have come from the Prague Treasury; Achille Seillière, Paris (until 1890); Duke of Marlborough, Blenheim Palace (until 1906); Widener Collection.

The title of the group has also been interpreted as "Glory Triumphing Over Vice." It was probably executed for the Emperor Rudolf II in whose service the sculptor worked after leaving Turin in 1593. Another group similar in design and of about the same dimensions, representing Samson fighting against a Philistine, was done by de Vries for the Emperor Mathias in 1612 (National Gallery, Edinburgh). The two may have been companion pieces; the correspondence of subject matter and dimensions would indicate such a relationship, although the difference in date may indicate that our example was originally thought of as an independent piece.

SELECTED REFERENCES: V. A. Ilg, Vienna *Jahrbuch,* I, 1883, p. 128; *La Chronique des arts et de la curiosité* (Seillière Sale), 1890, p. 155; C. Buchwald, *Adriaen de Vries,* Leipzig, 1899, pp. 54, 55, 100.

49. LORENZO BERNINI. ROMAN SCHOOL (1598-1680)

LOUIS XIV. A-62. Pages 152, 153. Bronze. H. 33⅛; W. 39⅜; D. 17 (0.842 x 1.000 x 0.432).

Collections: Said to have been in the collection of the Regent Philippe, Duc d' Orléans, Château of Saint-Cloud; E. Williamson, Paris; Sir Stuart Samuels, London; George J. Gould, Lakewood, New Jersey; Kress Collection.

In the spring of 1665, Bernini arrived in Paris on the invitation of Louis XIV to redesign the Louvre façade. His designs were ultimately rejected in favor of the classical colonnade attributed to Perrault which is still standing. By 1667, after his return to Rome, he was out of favor with the French court, and his journey to France might have been considered a failure were it not for the influence of his ideas and of the marble bust of the king which he left behind him. The marble, executed over the months of June through September of 1665, is now at Versailles. It proved to be extremely popular. Several casts in plaster were distributed in influential quarters soon after it was completed; one plaster is known to have been sent to the French Academy in Rome and another was presented by the king to his academy in Paris. A unique version in bronze is known to have survived to our day, and this is the superb *cire perdue,* which is preserved in the Kress Collection at the National Gallery of Art. Comparison of measurements and details indicates that this bronze is not a direct cast from the marble nor from one of the early plaster casts. On the other hand, the bronze in the main elements of its artistic effect is not far removed from Bernini: see for instance the purely Berninesque motive of the floating drapery. The style of modeling and certain technical peculiarities, however, correspond to seventeenth-century practice in France (see, for example, the bronze bust of Louis XIV after Coysevox, in the Wallace Collection, London). A bronze after the Bernini marble bust of the king, attributed to Derbais, is known to have been sent to Quebec in 1686 where it was put up in a public square of the city; the bust shortly after was taken down (Lami, *Dictionnaire des sculpteurs de l'école française sous le règne de Louis XIV,* pp. 145-146; P.-G. Roy, *Bulletin des recherches historiques* [Quebec], XXI, 1915, pp. 358-362). It is barely possible that the present bronze is the example sent back from Quebec. It is also possible that this magnificent bronze in the Kress Collection was made at the same time and presented to the king's family at Saint-Cloud where it is reported to have remained until the destruction of the Château in the Franco-Prussian war.

50. JEAN LOUIS LEMOYNE. FRENCH SCHOOL (1665-1755)

DIANA. A-127. Pages 154-157. Marble. H. (with plinth) 71¾; W. 30⅛; D. 22¾ (1.825 x 0.765 x 0.578). Signed: J. L. LEMOYNE · PARISINUS · FECIT · 1724.

Collections: Château de la Muette, near Paris; Rodolphe Kann, Paris (sold 1907); Widener Collection.

In 1710 Jean Louis Lemoyne was chosen with some of the most distinguished sculptors of his day to carve a figure for a group at the royal Château of Marly representing the nymphs of Diana. The group was broken up before the Revolution, and Lemoyne's statue disappeared. In 1724, however, he was commissioned to make a replica for the park of the Château de la Muette, near Paris. A drawing of the first version as it looked when still on view at Marly makes it possible to identify with certainty the present statue with the commission of 1724, in conformity with the inscribed date and signature (J. L. Lemoyne, not J. B. Lemoyne as indicated by Réau in his book referred to below). The title of "Diana" is a modern interpretation growing from the isolation of the figure from its original context as part of a group. It is mentioned in eighteenth-century descriptions as a "Companion of Diana."

SELECTED REFERENCES: Dézallier d'Argenville, *Voyage pittoresque des environs de Paris,* Paris, 1768, p. 15; L. Réau, *Les Lemoyne,* Paris, 1927, pp. 17, 34 (reproduces the available original manuscript sources in the Archives Nationales, Paris, including a relevant passage from an inventory of the sculpture at La Muette dated 1746 also printed in *Nouvelles archives de l'art français,* 1892).

51. CLODION (CLAUDE MICHEL). FRENCH SCHOOL (1738-1814)

MONUMENTAL URN. A-44. Pages 158, 159. Marble. H. 51¾; W. 38¼; D. 28¾ (1.31 x 0.971 x 0.73).

Collections: Demidoff, Palace of San Donato, Florence (sold 1880); Madame I. Perrier, Paris; Mellon Collection.

According to an unverified report this urn with its companion (A-43, signed and dated 1782) was intended for the gardens of Versailles. That not merely the design but the execution is by Clodion is indicated by two inferior versions (apparently of the period) now in the Huntington Art Gallery in San Marino, California. A terra-cotta study or version of one of the cartouche scenes, representing a mother-satyr with her child, was given in 1942 to the National Gallery of Art by Mrs. John H. Simpson.

SELECTED REFERENCES: *Vente de la Collection Demidoff,* Florence, 1880, pp. 24-25; H. Thirion, *Les Adam et Clodion,* Paris, 1885, p. 410; S. Lami, *Dictionnaire des sculpteurs de l'école française au XVIIIe siècle,* 1911, II, 156.

52-53. JEAN ANTOINE HOUDON. FRENCH SCHOOL (1741-1828)

ALEXANDRE BRONGNIARD. A-117. Pages 160-162. Marble. H. 15⁷⁄₁₆; W. 11⁵⁄₁₆; D. 7⁷⁄₁₆ (0.392 x 0.287 x 0.19). Signed: A. HOUDON, F. AN. 1777.

LOUISE BRONGNIARD. A-118. Pages 163, 164. Marble. H. 14¹³⁄₁₆; W. 9¹⁵⁄₁₆; D. 7¹¹⁄₁₆ (0.377 x 0.253 x 0.195).

Collections: Baron Jérome Pichon (great nephew and grandson of subjects), Joseph Bardac, Paris (before 1897); Widener Collection.

In 1777, Houdon exhibited busts of the young Brongniard children in the Salon. The catalogue, unfortunately, does not specify the material, whether marble or terra cotta or plaster. However, the material last named before the mention of the busts, is marble. It is quite possible, therefore, that our marble of the boy which is dated 1777 was exhibited at that time. The terra-cotta model, which preceded the marble, is in the Louvre, where it came with the terra-cotta model of the bust of Louise Brongniard directly from the Brongniard family. The two terra-cotta models were probably also shown in the Salon of 1777 under the title *Têtes d'Etude* (study-heads) hitherto unidentified.

There are several marble versions of the *Louise:* one in the Altman Collection in the Metropolitan Museum of Art, New York, another belonging to the Frank Collection in Paris, and the present example; still another belongs to Mr. Joseph Klein of Philadelphia. All except the first follow the terra cotta in the Louvre. The example in New York differs in costume; the little girl is shown with a turban-like headdress and a *fichu* around her neck and shoulders. As regards costume and also style of carving she is closest to the marble version of her brother Alexandre. In spite of the date inscribed on the back (1779; possibly a later addition) the Metropolitan example is the most likely of the three to have been shown in the Salon of 1777. Our example appears to be later in style and corresponds in handling of surfaces to Houdon's style of the 1780's (cf. his marbles of his own children). It is possible that the Brongniard family ordered this version; it corresponds very closely with the terra cotta which they owned and the lack of costume would fit the classicizing taste of the 1780's. The provenance of the piece is the same as that of the marble boy and goes back, in so far as it can be checked, to descendants of the subjects.

SELECTED REFERENCES: C. H. Hart and E. Biddle, *Jean Antoine Houdon,* Philadelphia, 1911, p. 19; G. Giacometti, *Le Vie et l'oeuvre de Houdon,* Paris, 1929, II, 21; L. Réau, *Houdon,* Paris, 1930, p. 122.

54-55. JEAN-BAPTISTE CARPEAUX. FRENCH SCHOOL (1827-1875)

GIRL WITH A SHELL. A-65. Pages 165, 167. Marble. H. 40¾; W. 16⅞; D. 20⁵⁄₁₆ (1.035 x 0.43 x 0.515). Signed: CARPEAUX, 1867.

THE NEAPOLITAN FISHERBOY. A-64. Page 166. Marble. H. 36¼; W. 16½; D. 18⁷⁄₁₆ (0.92 x 0.42 x 0.47). Signed: CARPEAUX, 1861.

Collections: Napoleon III and Empress Eugénie (acquired from the artist); Prince Victor Napoleon Bonaparte, Farnsborough, Hampshire, England; Kress Collection.

Although the two statues make a pair, they were executed at different times. The *Fisherboy* was begun by Carpeaux when he was still at the French Academy in Rome. The plaster (now in the Louvre) is dated 1857; a bronze version followed in 1859; this marble, completed two years later, was exhibited in the Salon of 1863 and in the Exposition Universelle of 1867. The *Girl with a Shell* was shown in the Salon of 1867 and was acquired by the Emperor in that year. The *Fisherboy* was bought by the Empress at the same time. They were taken by their owners into exile in England in 1871.

The artistic sources for the *Fisherboy* are in Rude's *Boy with a Tortoise* (Dijon) and in a remarkable combination of study from life and the Antique. The *Girl with a Shell* is related to the famous *Flore* by Carpeaux, on a pediment of the "New Louvre." The link between the Louvre figure and the present marble is a free-standing statue entitled *Flore:* a terra cotta was listed in 1927 as in the Maurice de Rothschild Collection, Paris; a later full-size white marble, inscribed "London, 1873" is in the Gulbenkian Collection, Paris, and a marble statuette is in the William Rockhill Nelson Collection, Kansas City. The girl's head is derived from a portrait of Anna Foucart, daughter of a close friend of the artist. Her features appear in a number of fancy-busts (examples in this country in the Boston Museum of Fine Arts and the National Collection of Fine Arts, Washington, D. C.).

SELECTED REFERENCES: P. Mantz, in *Gazette des Beaux-Arts,* XIII, 1876, pp. 603, 610; L. Riotor, *Carpeaux,* Paris (no date), pp. 37, 55, 63, 115; E. Sarradin, *Carpeaux,* Paris,

1927, pp. 10, 35-36, 38; L. Clément-Carpeaux, *La Verité sur l'oeuvre et la vie de J. B. Carpeaux,* Paris, 1934, pp. 76, 77, 81, 96, 109, 151, 161-162, 209.

56. AUGUSTE RODIN. FRENCH SCHOOL (1840-1917)

THE AGE OF BRONZE. A-74. Page 168. Bronze, dark patina with touches of light green and rust brown. H. 41; W. 14; D. 8⅝ (1.041 x 0.355 x 0.219). Signed at top of base: RODIN.

Collections: Simpson, New York (acquired directly from the artist); gift of Mrs. John W. Simpson.

Rodin worked on the original life-size version from October 1875 to March 1877. It was exhibited at the *Salon* of that year. Adverse critics at that time, curiously enough, accused Rodin of having molded the figure from life. Over the succeeding years, the figure has proved one of the most admired of all Rodin's designs. Several reductions were made by Rodin; two are listed by Bénédite but both are smaller than the present example. This is not a mechanical reduction of the large figure of 1877, but modeled completely afresh, in the freer style of about 1900. A first-hand report states that Rodin personally supervised the process of patination.

REFERENCE: L. Bénédite, *Rodin,* London, 1924, p. 25.